MARX VIA PROCESS

Whitehead's Potential Contribution to Marxian Social Theory

Russell L. Kleinbach

Philadelphia College of Textiles and Science

UNIVERSITY
PRESS OF
AMERICA

Copyright © 1982 by Russell L. Kleinbach

University Press of America,Inc.™
P.O. Box 19101, Washington, D.C. 20036

Printed in the United States of America

ISBN: 0-8191-2274-2 (Perfect)
0-8191-2273-4 (Case)

Library of Congress Number: 81-40667

This study is dedicated to

Paul K. Deats, Jr.

my advisor, teacher and colleague
with whom I struggled, and shared the tasks of
learner, teacher, and committee member

Acknowledgements

I wish to acknowledge with appreciation Carl Bangs who introduced me to Alfred North Whitehead, the people of Viet Nam who introduced me to Marxian social praxis, and Paul K. Deats, Jr., who was my Ph.D. advisor; without them this book would never have been written.

I wish to sincerely thank Deborah Baskin, Samuel Z. Klausner and especially Donna Trieger, without whose encouragement and help this book would never have been published.

The manuscript was originally presented as my doctoral dissertation at Boston University in the field of Social Ethics.

Permission has been granted by the respective publishers for the quotations which have been used from the following copyrighted material.

Althusser, Louis. For Marx. New York: Vintage Books, 1970.

Bottomore, T.B., ed. Karl Marx: Early Writings. New York: McGraw-Hill Book Company, 1964.

Easton, Loyd D. and Guddat, Kurt H. Translators and editors, Writings of the Young Marx on Philosophy and Society. New York: Doubleday & Co.; Anchor Books, 1967.

Engels, Frederick. Anti-Duhring. New York: International Publishers, 1939; New World Paperbacks, 1972.

Gramsci, Antonio. Selections From the Prison Notebooks. New York: International Publishers, 1971.

Habermas, Jurgen. Knowledge and Human Interests. Boston: Beacon Press, 1971.

Korsch, Karl. Karl Marx. New York: Russell & Russell, 1963.

Lenin, V.I. Materialism and Empirio-Criticism. New York: International Publishers, 1927.

Macpherson, C.B. Democratic Theory: Essays in Retrieval. Oxford: Clarendon Press, 1973.

Marcuse, Herbert. Reason and Revolution. New York: Humanities Press, 1954.

Marx, Karl. Capital. Volume 1. Translated from the Third German Edition by Samuel Moore and Edward Aveling, edited by Frederick Engels. New York: International Publishers, 1967.

_____. Grundrisse: Foundations of the Critique of Political Economy. Translated by Martin Nicolaus. Middlesex, England: Penguin Books, 1973. Permission granted by Random House, Inc., New York.

_____. Poverty of Philosophy. New York: International Publishers; New World Paperbacks, 1963.

_____. The German Ideology. Edited by C.J. Arthur. New York: International Publishers; New World Paperbacks, 1970.

Ollmann, Bertell. Alienation: Marx's Conception of Man in a Capitalist Society. Cambridge, England: Cambridge University Press, 1971.

Schram, Stuart R. The Political Thought of Mao Tse-Tung. Revised and enlarged ed. New York: Praeger Publishers, 1969.

Selsam, Howard, Goldway, David, and Martel, Harry, eds. Dynamic of Social Change. New York: International Publishers, 1970; New World Paperbacks, 1973.

Whitehead, Alfred North. Adventures of Ideas. New York: Macmillan, 1933; Free Press, 1967. Permission granted by Macmillan.

_____. Process and Reality. New York: Macmillan Company, 1929; New York: Harper Torchbooks, 1960. Permission granted by Macmillan.

_____. Science and the Modern World. New York: Macmillan, 1925; Free Press, 1967. Permission granted by Macmillan.

TABLE OF CONTENTS

ABBREVIATIONS OF SOURCE

In this study reference is made to certain of White-head's and Marx's works by means of the following standard abbreviations:

ALFRED NORTH WHITEHEAD

AI   Adventures of Ideas. New York: Macmillan, 1933; Free Press, 1967.

FR   The Function of Reason. Princeton: Princeton University Press, 1929; Boston: Beacon Press, 1958.

MT   Modes of Thought. New York: Macmillan, 1938; Free Press, 1968.

PR   Process and Reality. New York: Macmillan, 1929; New York: Harper Torchbooks, 1960.

SMW   Science and the Modern World. New York: Macmillan, 1925; Free Press, 1967.

SYM   Symbolism. New York: Macmillan, 1927; Capricorn Books, 1959.

KARL MARX

Capital   Capital. Volumes 1, 2, & 3. Translated from the third German edition by Samuel Moore and Edward Aveling, edited by Frederick Engels. New York: International Publishers, 1967.

CHR   Contribution to the Critique of Hegel's Philosophy of Right: Introduction, in Karl Marx: Early Writings. Translated and edited by T.B. Bottomore. New York: McGraw-Hill, 1964, pp. 41-59.

Critique   A Contribution to the Critique of Political Economy. Edited by Maurice Dobb. New York: International Publishers, New World Paperbacks, 1970.

CGP   Critique of the Gotha Programme. New York: International Publishers; Little Marx Library, 1966.

EPM   Economic and Philosophical Manuscripts, in
Karl Marx: Early Writings. Translated by
T.B. Bottomore. New York: McGraw-Hill,
1964.

18th   The 18th Brumaire of Louis Bonaparte.
Brumaire New York: International Publishers; New
World Paperbacks, 1970.

Grundrisse Grundrisse: Foundations of the Critique of
Political Economy. Translated by Martin
Nicolaus. Middlesex, England: Penguin
Books, 1973.

HF   The Holy Family. Moscow: Foreign Language
Publishing House, 1956.

JQ   On the Jewish Question, in Karl Marx: Early
Writings. Translated and edited by T.B.
Bottomore. New York: McGraw-Hill, 1964,
pp. 1-40.

PP   Poverty of Philosophy. New York: International Publishers; New World Paperbacks,
1963.

TF   Theses on Feuerbach, in Karl Marx: Selected
Writings in Sociology and Social Philoso-
phy. Translated by T.B. Bottomore. New
York: McGraw-Hill, 1956, pp. 67-69.

PREFACE

Marxist theory has become a powerful economic, political, social and cultural force in the world. It is not a finished theory but an emergent theory. It has its base in the writings of Marx and Engels but has been, and is being, developed and practiced by many theorists, statesmen, and revolutionaries throughout the world. As an emergent theory and practice, addressing the varied questions and conditions which it does, it is not without unresolved problems and divergent perspectives and emphases. Some of these problems and differences are methodological, some are theoretical, some are a matter of emphasis, and some are a result of Marxist theory having its linguistic, conceptual and empirical roots in nineteenth century Europe. It is the hypothesis of this study that some or many of these problems may be clarified, by-passed and/or resolved by restructuring the nineteenth century linguistic and conceptual idiom into modern linguistic and conceptual paradigms, or at least by understanding the nineteenth century idiom in its historical context and translating its meaning into modern idiom for utilization and application. This process would also include some substantive utilization of the modern paradigms and idiom.

In an effort to operationalize this hypothesis, and in the hope that a small contribution might be made to the larger theoretical problem, i.e., unresolved issues in Marxist theory, I will address in depth one aspect of the larger theoretical concern. In this context then, this study is concerned with the dynamic coincidence of social existence, creating humans and their consciousness, and of human conscious activity creating social existence. In particular it focuses on the human capacity, and its limits, to intervene, i.e., give direction, consciously and creatively to the relatively determined process of human history.

INTRODUCTION

A. The Problem and its Significance

The specific problem of this study is to analyze the category of consciousness as developed in Alfred North Whitehead's philosophy of organism and to explore critically the possible contribution of this category to Marxist theory at the point where Marxist theory deals with the capacity of humans to intervene creatively and consciously in the process of human history. It is important to note that the category "Marxist theory" as used in this study does not refer to a closed or finished theory or system, or to the theory of only Marx and Engels, but rather to the continually developing political, economic and social theory which is rooted in the writings of Marx and Engels.

It will also become apparent that the primary source for Whitehead's contribution to this problem will come from Process and Reality, and not from the growing number of books and studies on Whitehead and process philosophy. This is true because to my knowledge neither Whitehead nor his students have developed the implications of efficient causation, i.e., the "materialist" side of his scheme, in balance with his "idealism," as found in final causation and developed in Adventures of Ideas. Most particularly this has not been done with respect to its implications for social-political theory.

The problem requires these tasks: 1. I will analyze the understanding of consciousness in the philosophy of organism. 2. I will analyze the human capacity to intervene consciously and creatively in the process of human history, as represented in the writings of Marx and a representative sample of Marxist theories. 3. I will explore critically the possible implications of Whitehead's understanding of consciousness for the development of Marxist theory at the point where it deals with the capacity of humans to intervene consciously in the process of history. This task assumes that "Marxist theory" is not "finished," and that some aspects of Whitehead's theory may possibly contribute to the ongoing Marxist discussion, for example, at these points: (i) materialist-idealist and freedom-determinism questions, (ii) epistemology, (iii) Marxist normative judgments, (iv) the relation of existence to consciousness, and (v) the narrow focus of a "materialist" perspective.

1

Most Marxist theorists are determinists up to a point. But most if not all of them give some leeway for humans to interfere consciously with their history though they differ on the degree of freedom and the weighting and function of the other determining factors which influence human history (i.e., geographical-eco-logical environment, structures of productive and social relations, technology, and culture). I have chosen to bring to this problem as it has emerged in Marxist theory Whitehead's understanding of consciousness for the following reasons:

1. As I will seek to demonstrate, within develop-ing Marxist theory there have been and are apparently conflicting positions and statements by Marx and Marxists on aspects of this question. The apparent conflicts are as numerous in Marx as in Marxist theorists. This study will seek to demonstrate unity as well as diversity on these issues. The range of positions among Marxist theorists include: (i) the "techno-environmental and techno-economic determinism" of Marvin Harris,[1] (ii) the interpretation of Marx by Louis Althusser, which empha-sizes the materialist and economic analyses in Marx,[2] (iii) important essays by Mao Tse-Tung: "On Contradic-tion," "On Practice," and "Combat Liberalism" among others,[3] (iv) Bertell Ollman's explication of Marx as a relational thinker in Alienation,[4] and (v) some of the writings of Herbert Marcuse[5] and Jurgen Habermas,[6] and similar but earlier and less psychological work of George Lukacs,[7] Karl Korsch,[8] and Antonio Gramsci.[9] The last five of these theorists can be placed on the more liberal "humanist" end of the spectrum and they draw heavily on the early writings of Marx as represented in "The Theses on Feuerbach," The Economic and Philosophical Manuscripts and the Contribution to the Critique of Hegel's Philosophy of Right. The work of Mao Tse-Tung and Ollman reflects a cross section of Marx's early and later writings, and theorists such as Harris and Althusser draw more on the writings of the "mature" Marx represented by the following well known passage:

> In the social production which men carry on they enter into definite relations that are indispensable and independent of their will; these relations of production correspond to a definite stage of development of their material powers of production. The sum total of these relations of production constitutes the eco-nomic structure of society--the real founda-tions, on which rise legal and political super-structures and to which correspond definite

forms of social consciousness. The mode of production in material life determines the general character of the social, political, and spiritual processes of life. It is not the consciousness of men that determines their existence, but, on the contrary, their social existence determines their consciousness.[10]

2. It is important for radical theorists in the Marxist tradition to clarify the issue(s) of the relationship of consciousness to existence, particularly as we search for an increasingly enabling theoretical understanding of our capacity to intervene consciously and creatively in the process of our own history. What should be helpful to this effort is a developed theoretical statement which analyzes the potentiality, limits, relations to other determining factors, and timing of conscious intervention, which persons or groups must take into account if they wish to intervene in their own history. Whitehead's analysis may incorporate into the Marxist discussion a conception of the relationship of consciousness to existence which is developed in the tradition of relational thinkers such as Spinoza, Leibniz and Hegel, out of a modern physical science and early twentieth century philosophical tradition, and within an inclusive, holistic, and non-dualistic worldview.

3. I believe Whitehead's understanding of consciousness can make a fruitful contribution to Marxist theory because Whitehead incorporates within his understanding of consciousness the time, place and conditions wherein emerges the capacity to make judgments for the future. These judgments use the determinant data of the past and the present, and include an awareness of the relative determinedness of the process of history.[11] The judgments also include an awareness (negative judgments) of what the past and the present are not, and an awareness of the possibilities of what might be (PR 245).

Images of the possibilities of what might be are drawn from the exclusiveness of what is, creative imagination, and knowledge of the nature of reality. This understanding of consciousness provides the possibility of contributing to Marxist theory some theoretical statements which help to clarify how and when persons and groups can intervene and direct the relatively determined historical process of which they are a part.

3

The implication of this study is the possibility that, on this question, Whitehead's developed theory may contribute to Marxist theory in the following ways: (i) by enabling the materialist-idealist and freedom-determinism questions to be answered or by-passed, by accounting for all of the factors in one coherent scheme, (ii) by further developing the Marxist epistemology in a way which affirms a <u>direct</u> human relationship to the real world and also accounts for error in human conceptualization,   (iii)   by adding the understanding that the quality of subjective experience is the locus of value, and by adding an emphasis on the social nature of reality to the Marxist concern for human development and the overcoming   of human alienation,   thus clarifying and balancing the implicit normative referent in Marxist theory, (iv) by providing a theoretical scheme which accounts for and makes mutually supportive, the dual affirmation that social existence determines consciousness and that consciously willed action can determine social existence, and (v) by utilizing the notion of compatibility, derived from Whitehead, in conjunction with his more developed theory of causation, to make the "materialistic" focus more holistic.

B.   Limitations

This study limits its focus to an exploration and analysis of the understanding of consciousness in Whitehead's philosophy of organism, and to its possible value to Marxist theory.

Analysis of and references to the place of the human capacity to intervene consciously in the process of history in the writings of Marx and the representative sample of Marxist theorists will be critical and comparative. These references will be limited but complete enough to enable an understanding of the role of the capacity for intervention in the theorists discussed. This limitation is spelled out further in the explanation below of my use of a representative sample as a method in the study.

To save repetition I want to make it clear at the beginning of the study that I am aware that there is much in Marxist theory that is subject to continuing argument and divergent interpretation. There is no attempt to ignore or simplify these issues. Thus it deserves emphasis that "Marxist theory" as used in this study refers to my interpretation of Marxist theory. My interpretation is based on my study of Marx's writings and the writings of a representative sample of Marxist theorists at the points where these writings address the problem of this study. In my use of the term "Marxist theory" I do not mean to imply that there are not genuinely conflicting interpretations of Marx or that there are not Marxists and Marx-theorists who will challenge my interpretation.

There will be references to the points of consonance and divergence between Marxist theory and Whitehead's philosophy. It is not intended that these references be complete nor that this study establish that the two schemes as a whole are consonant or dissonant systems. It is intended that these references be complete only insofar as they are relevant to the problem of this study.

Finally, this study is limited to the potential contribution of Whitehead's process theory as developed in Process and Reality to Marxist social theory and will not address the question of whether or not Whitehead's process theory is the only or best process-relational model for the task of addressing certain problems in Marxist theory. I will focus solely on the potential contribution to Marxist theory of this one theory.

C. Methods

The study will utilize the methods of analysis, criticism and representative sample. The major criterion for criticism will be coherence.

Analytical: The study will attempt to explain the relation of the capacity to intervene consciously in human history as developed in Whitehead's philosophy of organism to this capacity in Marxist theory.

Critical: The study will explore critically the implications of Whitehead's understanding for Marxist theory. Whitehead writes that speculative philosophy "is the endeavor to frame a coherent, logical, necessary system of general ideas in terms of which every element of our experience can be interpreted [PR 4]." This study deals with only a limited area of our experience, but it will attempt to be both logical and coherent.

'Coherence,' as here employed, means that the fundamental ideas, in terms of which the scheme is developed, presuppose each other so that in isolation they are meaningless. This requirement does not mean that they are definable in terms of each other; it means that what is indefinable in one such notion cannot be abstracted from its relevance to the other notions [PR 5].[12]

This is important because both Whitehead and Marx are systematic and "coherent" theorists. "The fundamental concepts of both thinkers are systematic concepts, as such, concepts that achieve their precise meaning only in their niche within a systematic scheme."[13] It will be shown however that the major possible contributions of Whitehead's theory result from the superior "coherence" achieved in his language and categories.

Representative sample: I will attempt to make the study both manageable and specific by selecting and focusing on the writings (in addition to Marx's) of several Marxist theorists, who, as I will attempt to demonstrate, represent the range of Marxist thinking on this issue. Theorists will be used at those points where their writings are particularly relevant to the study by virtue of their discussion of the problem and related issues. As explained earlier in the Introduction, the category "Marxist theory," as used in this study, does not refer to a closed or finished theory or system, or to the theory of only Marx and Engels, but to the continually developing political, economic and social theory which is rooted in the writings of Marx and Engels and which has continued to develop in the writings of many theorists since Marx wrote. My concern is not to define Marxist theory, to deal exclusively with the writings of Marx and Engels, or to find a consensus among Marxist theorists. The method of the study is a struggle with Marxist theory as rooted in the writings of Marx and developing from and in the writings of a range (representative sample) of Marxist theorists. The theorists discussed are not necessarily representative of Marxist theory on all issues but they do represent the issues, in Marxist theory, and the range of positions respective to the issues, with which this study is concerned. The study will not attempt to solve these questions. The purpose of the study is to raise the questions and to explore possible ways these questions may be by-passed,[14] given clarity and/or answered if they are addressed with the assistance of the process paradigm.

D. Previous Research

I have not located any studies which duplicate this one.

Allison H. Johnson has published two books, White-head's Philosophy of Civilization[15] and Whitehead's Theory of Reality,[16] which are of help in the analysis of Whitehead. The same can be said for The Philosophy of Alfred North Whitehead, edited by Paul Arthur Schilpp.[17] Of particular interest in this volume is Joseph Needham's essay,[18] in which he points out the consonance between Whitehead and Marx in several areas, e.g., (i) they share a dialectical and organic conception of nature, (ii) both are naturalists concerned with levels of complexity and organization of reality, and (iii) both understand mentality as based in complex material reality. This study concurs with these conclusions and will develop and document these points in each theorist.

Several dissertations have been written which are also very helpful for the Whitehead section, but none of these directly address the problem of the study.

Several of the Marxist theorists deal implicitly, and a few explicitly, with the capacity to intervene in history, but I have not located any analysis of this capacity which utilizes Whitehead's understanding of consciousness. Ollman's Alienation is the work closest to the concern of this study. Ollman is concerned to show that Marx is really a relational theorist, which I do not attempt to do. Furthermore, there are aspects of process theory, e.g., the theory of causation, which are very important, but not found in Marx, nor dealt with by Ollman.

Jorge V. Pixley, in the article to which I have already referred, attempts to demonstrate three things: (i) that there is no fundamental incompatibility between Whitehead and Marx, "or more exactly, between their conceptual systems," (ii) that "Marx's atheism is not a necessary ingredient for his conceptual system," and (iii) that Marx and Whitehead are in basic agreement on their understanding of the role of ideas and final causation.[19] This study differs in that (i) I will not be attempting to show that there is no incompatibility between Whitehead and Marx, but to show ways in which Whitehead's theory might contribute to Marxist theory in a particular area and (ii) I will acknowledge that White-head's theism and his notion of objects as "eternal" conflict radically with Marxist theory and I will not try

7

to demonstrate that theism is a possible contribution to Marxist theory.

Howard L. Parsons has written a short but helpful essay[20] in which he briefly points out and illustrates how Marx and Whitehead "complement one another in a sort of dialectical tension."[21] He sees both Marx and Whitehead as holistic theorists with "quite similar" outlooks on major issues such as (i) the idealism-materialism issue,[22] (ii) their social concern for human fulfillment,[23] (iii) the theory that humans come out of nature and in turn shape their environment,[24] and (iv) the "fact that each by different routes reached the same general world view-- [Whitehead] socialistic naturalism, [and Marx] naturalistic socialism,..."[25] Parsons argues, however, that the complementing character of the human community and the community of nature has yet to be developed; that is to say, it has not yet been shown "how the community of man, the community of nature, and the community of man with nature might be reinforced and enhanced."[26]

This study is in basic agreement with most of Parsons' essay and is in some ways an expansion of his position; that is to say, in this study I will describe in detail each theorist's position on these issues, as they relate to the problem of the study, and then focus on how Whitehead's developed theory can complement and contribute to making Marxist theory a more adequate social theory.

Format: The study is structured in a format which includes an introduction, three substantive chapters and a summary of conclusions. In Chapter I, I will attempt to explore the understanding of consciousness in the philosophy of organism, in language which will facilitate the integration, or translation if necessary, of Whitehead's categories and insights into language useful in social theory. This chapter will not provide an introduction to the whole of Whitehead's philosophy but will have the task of setting forth an understanding of the category of consciousness in relation to other related categories in Whitehead's philosophy of organism and to language of social theory. In Chapter II, I will discuss Marxist theory in the context of the question of human conscious intervention in the historical process. I will discuss relevant Marxist categories, assumptions, methods, and conclusions; and I will make note of divergent Marxist positions and of parallels between Marxist theory and Whitehead's philosophy. Throughout Chapter II, I will make use of Marx's writings and extensive references to the writings of the representative sample of Marxist theorists. Thus the purpose of the chapter will not be to pose the problems and questions in Marxist theory with which this study is concerned but, as a parallel to Chapter I on Whitehead, the task of Chapter II will be to set forth the relevant Marxist theoretical categories and scheme. In Chapter III, I will refer to the material in the first two chapters and I will discuss at length six important problem areas in Marxist theory. All of these six problems or questions are fundamentally important aspects of the concern of this study, i.e., a theoretical discussion of the human capacity to intervene consciously in the historical process. I will not attempt a resolution of these questions but I will raise the questions and explore the possible ways these questions may be clarified, by-passed and/or answered when addressed with the assistance of an undertaking and/or application of the process paradigm. The questions discussed will include the idealism-materialism problem, the freedom-determinism question, the epistemological question, the normative referent for guiding conscious intervention in the historical process, the timing of effective intervention, and the question of compatibility between desired experiences and social environment. The Conclusion is a summary of the findings and conclusions of the study.

Preface and Introduction

1. Marvin Harris, The Rise of Anthropological Theory (New York: Thomas Y. Crowell Company, 1968), p. 4.

2. Louis Althusser, For Marx (New York: Vintage Books, 1970), see for example, pp. 107-111.

3. Stuart Schram, The Political Thought of Mao Tse-Tung, Revised ed. (New York: Praeger Publishers, 1969).

4. Bertell Ollman, Alienation: Marx's Conception of Man in Capitalist Society (Cambridge, England: Cambridge University Press, 1971).

5. Herbert Marcuse, Reason and Revolution (New York: Humanities Press, 1954).

6. Jurgen Habermas, Knowledge and Human Interests (Boston: Beacon Press, 1971). Theory and Practice (Boston: Beacon Press, 1973).

7. George Lukacs, History and Class Consciousness (Cambridge, Massachusetts: MIT Press, 1971).

8. Karl Korsch, Karl Marx (New York: Russell and Russell, 1963). Marxism and Philosophy (London: NBL, 1970).

9. Antonio Gramsci, Letters from Prison (New York: Harper and Row, 1973); and Selections from the Prison Notebooks (New York: International Publishers, 1971).

10. Karl Marx, "Preface to Critique of Political Economy," in Karl Marx and Friedrich Engels, Basic Writings on Politics and Philosophy, ed. Lewis S. Feuer (New York: Doubleday, 1959), p. 43.

11. Alfred North Whitehead, Process and Reality (New York: Macmillan Company, 1929; New York: Harper Torchbooks, 1960), p. 309, hereafter referred to as PR.

12. This definition of "coherence" is not meant to be a normative or definitive definition of the category: For example, it is not the same as that given by Edgar Brightman.

13. Jorge V. Pixley, "Whitehead y Marx Sobre la Dinamica de la Historia," Dialogos 7 (University of Puerto Rico) (April-June, 1970); 86-87 (my translation).

14. "By-pass" as used in this study refers to the possibility of reorganizing the categories of a problem in such a way that the problem as understood in the past is no longer a problem and yet the categories are all accounted for.

15. A.H. Johnson, Whitehead's Philosophy of Civilization (New York: Dover Publications, 1962).

16. A.H. Johnson, Whitehead's Theory of Reality (New York: Dover Publications, 1962).

17. Paul Arthur Schilpp, ed. The Philosophy of Alfred North Whitehead (LaSalle, Illinois: Open Court, 1951).

18. Joseph Needham, "A Biologist's View of Whitehead's Philosophy," in The Philosophy of Alfred North Whitehead, ed. Paul Arthur Schilpp (LaSalle, Illinois: Open Court, 1951), pp. 241-72.

19. Pixley, "Whitehead y Marx Sobre la Dinamica de la Historia," pp. 106-7.

20. Howard L. Parsons, "History as Viewed by Marx and Whitehead," Christian Scholar L (1967): 273-89.

21. Ibid., p. 273.

22. Ibid., p. 275.

23. Ibid., p. 284.

24. Ibid.

25. Ibid., p. 288.

26. Ibid.

CHAPTER I

THE NOTION OF CONSCIOUSNESS AS DEVELOPED
IN WHITEHEAD'S PHILOSOPHY OF ORGANISM

The task of this chapter is to explicate the understanding of consciousness in the philosophy of organism, in language which will facilitate the integration, or translation if necessary, of some of Whitehead's insights into language useful in social theory.[1]

The task of this study is not to provide an introduction to the whole of Whitehead's philosophy, or to provide a definition of all of his categories; both of these tasks have been done adequately elsewhere.[2] Holding in mind the concern to understand how and when persons can intervene consciously in the process of their own history, the task of this study is to understand the category of consciousness[3] in relation to other related categories in Whitehead's philosophy of organism and to the language of social theory. I will discuss especially the following categories: (i) the ontological principle, (ii) actual entity, (iii) efficient causation, (iv) final causation, (v) self-causation, (vi) negative judgments, (vii) speculative philosophy, (viii) propositions, (ix) presentational immediacy, and (x) compatibility.

A. Consciousness in the Philosophy of Organism

1. Consciousness in Relation
to the Ontological Principle

For Whitehead the ontological principle is the principle of causation and accountability: "there is nothing which floats into the world from nowhere [PR 373]." Whitehead states the principle thus:

> That every condition to which the process of becoming conforms in any particular instance, has its reason either in the character of some actual entity in the actual world of that concrescence, or in the character of the subject which is in the process of concrescence.
>
> This category of explanation is termed the 'ontological principle.' It could also be termed the 'principle of efficient, and final, causation.' This ontological principle means that actual entities are the only reasons; so

13

that to search for a <u>reason</u> is to search for one
or more actual entities [PR 36-37].

If we understand the term "condition" used in this quotation to include consciousness, then we can say that when
a person experiences consciousness, that experience, including its content, has a reason or cause. That reason,
or reasons, can be found in the "actual world" of the
person, or in the experiencing person. The term "actual"
here refers to the "stubborn facts,"[4] both physical and
conceptual, of the relevant past (PR 197).

This principle of causation is fundamental to Whitehead. His own use of it here is clear on the point that
efficient causation is found in the actual world of the
person and that final causation is found within the
experiencing person; but what is missing in the above
quotation is the distinction between "final causation"
and "self-causation" or "<u>causa</u> <u>sui</u> [PR 135]." Whitehead
often combines or merges these two concepts when he uses
the term final causation. This distinction will become
clear when we discuss the categories of "eternal object"
and "subjective aim."

Thus according to Whitehead's ontological principle,[5] consciousness has its reason, or cause, in the modes
of efficient, final and self-causation, within the experience of an actual occasion.

2. Consciousness in Relation to the Category of Actual Entity

"Actual entities," also termed "actual occasions,"
are the "...final real things of which the world is made
up [PR 27]." They differ among themselves, and they have
"gradations of importance, and diversities of function
[PR 28]." Whitehead also calls them "drops of experience." As the term which he uses for an "actuality," it
can refer to a stone, a flower, an animal, a person, or a
community of persons, at any concrete (actual or emerging)
moment of its duration of life.[6] "For example, in the life
of man is an historic route of actual occasions which in
a marked degree . . . inherit from each other [PR 137]."
And we should add that in a marked degree each of these
occasions in the "historic route" inherits, via efficient
causation, from the other actual occasions in the person's
actual environment.

While Whitehead at times refers to the actual entity as having a threefold character (PR 135), he develops a fourfold character for it: (i) it has the character given for it by its past or actual world, including both physical and conceptual data, (ii) it has its subjective character, i.e., its decision-making or self-causing character, (iii) it has the character of "feeling" the lure of its chosen ideals,[7] and (iv) it has the "superjective" character which is its character as "actual" efficient data for future actual entities. Considering a conscious moment, or occasion, in a person's life, this scheme enables us to understand the following: (i) the person is a product of, i.e., brought forth out from, his/her physical and conceptual past, or social environment, (ii) the person is a conscious, feeling subject, who is deciding what he/she will become within the bounds of the past and the possibilities of the present and the future, (iii) the person is responding not only to the "vector" force of his/her past but to the lure of his/her chosen and inherited ideals, and (iv) the person is a "subject" who will become "objective," i.e., when the conscious moment has happened and it has become "past," it will have become objective data for future occasions in the life of this person, and for other occasions in its future.[8]

The initial phase of each emergent actual occasion is its coming forth out of its causal past as a recipient of efficient causation.

3. Consciousness in Relation to the Givenness of History, i.e., Efficient Causation

Efficient causation is the term used by Whitehead to speak of the effectively causal influence which the environment of the actual world has upon whoever and whatever emerges in the present and in the future. For Whitehead the "actual" world is the already world, it is the realm of the givens and of "stubborn fact."[9] The actual world is the only world out of which anything can arise or emerge. It provides the building blocks and forms, or the data (both physical and conceptual), out of which anything can arise or emerge, and out of which anything new must be created. Thus ". . . every actual entity springs from that universe which there is for it. Causation is nothing else than one outcome of the principle that every actual entity has to house its actual world [PR 124]."

15

For Whitehead, the present and future actual entities are created out of the material of their past actual world and thus house that world, but every actual entity "springs" from that universe which there is for it.[10] Here the term "springs" refers to the combined force of both the past and the present in the present; for although the past actual world is "objective," "given" and "stubborn fact," like bricks for a future wall, the past, i.e., the actual world (in the context of the emergent present) is not inert, it is not just there, it has conceptual and physical actuality and specificity, which are transferred to the present, or inherited via "feelings" felt by a subject or person.[11] "Feeling" in this sense is ". . . the appropriation of some elements in the universe to be components in the real internal constitution of its subject. The elements are the initial data; they are what the feeling feels [PR 353]." Feelings (also termed "emotional feelings," or "prehensions") transfer the past, or cause, into the present subject, or effect, with a "vector" character (PR 363-64). It is a "feeling from the cause which acquires the subjectivity of the new effect without loss of its original subjectivity in the cause [PR 363]."

> In the phraseology of physics, this primitive experience is 'vector feeling,' that is to say, feeling from a beyond which is determinate and pointing to a beyond which is to be determined. But the feeling is subjectively rooted in the immediacy of the present occasion: it is what the occasion feels for itself, as derived from the past and as merging into the future [PR 247].

The "beyond" in the above quotation refers to an actual entity's immediate relevant past and to its total conceptual and physical environment. The beyond is determinate, that is to say, it is the "already" "stubborn fact" which is determining the emerging subject's experience of becoming what it is becoming.[12] This is not to say that it is the only causal force, since we are referring only to efficient causation and not yet to self or final causation. The subject is experiencing, in the present, what it has derived from the past, and that with which it is creating itself, a self which when actualized will in turn be objective "vector" data for occasions in the future.

Whitehead illustrates efficient causation and the vector character of the past/environment in very concrete terms.

16

> The datum transmitted from the stone becomes
> the touch-feeling in the hand, but it preserves
> the vector-character of its origin from the
> stone. The touch-feeling in the hand with this
> vector origin from the stone is transmitted to
> the percipient in the brain [PR 183].

The "stone" in this quotation is part of the "beyond" and part of the "past" of the person. It is objective and in a sense just there, yet when felt by the person it becomes an ". . . element of the real internal constitution [PR 353]" of the person, that is to say, the person is now who he/she is, and not someone else because of the stone's ingression into his/her experience.

The stone to be "felt" via efficient causation need not be touched, it may be inherited directly by any of the senses, i.e., smell, hearing, sight, etc. In each of these modes the ". . . relevance of the vector character of the external inheritance . . ." will still be preserved (PR 182).

It is also important to note in this context that "in the final percipient any conscious feeling of the primitive emotional functioning of the sensum is often entirely absent. But this is not always the case; . . . [PR 480]." That is to say, a person's environment, i.e., past, can have a vector influence in one's experience and in who one becomes without this process entering consciousness. In fact, as I will point out later, consciousness only arises in a late derivative phase of some actual entities.

The implication of this discussion for social theory[13] is that all things which we hear, see, touch, smell, and/or with which we come in contact, consciously or unconsciously, causally determine what we will experience and who or what we will become, both for ourselves and for those occasions which we in turn influence. This will become clearer when I discuss further the concept of efficient causation.

Remembering that efficient causation is only one of Whitehead's three abstract interrelated modes of causation, we can discuss the two ways that efficient causation differs from mechanistic determinism.[14] First, efficient causation is an organic relationship, not an atomistic subject-predicate mode of causation. Second, what is given and inherited from our environment is both conceptual and physical. In the philosophy of organism the stubborn facts of our environment are not atoms or

17

subjects acting upon or against other atoms or subjects. It is true that the data of our causal environment are given; it (our environment) does not in itself change since it already is, and thus it cannot act as a subject can act. To describe the relations between our environment and ourselves Whitehead uses the language of both emotion and physical science.

> The direct perception whereby the datum in the immediate subject is inherited from the past can thus, under an abstraction, be conceived as the transference of throbs of emotional energy, clothed in the specific forms provided by sensa [PR 178].

> Emotional feeling is still subject to the third meta-physical principle, that to be 'something' is 'to have the potentiality for acquiring real unity with other entities.' Hence, 'to be a real component of an actual entity' is in some way 'to realize this potentiality.' Thus 'emotion' is 'emotional feeling;' and 'what is felt' is the presupposed vector situation. In physical science this principle takes the form which should never be lost sight of in fundamental speculation, that scalar quantities are constructs derivative from vector quantities. In more familiar language, this principle can be expressed by the statement that the notion of 'passing on' is more fundamental than that of a private individual fact. In the abstract language here adopted for metaphysical statement, 'passing on' becomes 'creativity,' in the dictionary sense of the verb creare, 'to bring forth, beget, produce' [PR 324].

For Whitehead, concepts (which are almost images) like "throbs of emotional energy," "emotional energy," "vector," and "passing on," while not as exact as atomistic language (with subjects and predicates), are more accurate to our experience of reality in both its mental and material aspects.

However, only in abstraction do we speak of the past in terms of "throbs of emotional energy," "vector" or "passing on," for these are statements about an environment which is in the presence of an emerging experiencing subject or person who when actualized will also become a past for a future. This language has meaning only if we are speaking of history and environment as relative to and related internally to the persons, things, and events in the present,[15] with the assumption that the present will become the data for future actual entities.

To speak of "organism" does not mean that actual occasions or persons lose their individuality or their subjectivity, rather it means a linguistic and conceptual shift from describing "attributes of physical bodies," to describing the "forms of internal relationships between actual occasions, and within actual occasions [PR 471]." This change of thought Whitehead calls the shift from materialism to "organic realism" in physical science, and is "the displacement of the notion of static stuff by the notion of fluent energy [PR 471]."[16] This change of thought applied to social theory means (in the context of a discussion of efficient causation) a discussion of the internal relationship between persons' present physical, emotional and conceptual experiences, and all of the actual occasions in their environmental and personal past. In terms of social theory it says that all of our physical, social and cultural environment is determinant of who we are, and comes throbbing into our experience whether we are ready or not, or conscious or not. In this mode of causation we as individuals are created out of and by the force of the physical and conceptual data of our past and environment. It is the real potentiality of our past and environment finding real unity in our present existence by creatively bringing forth our present existence. Yet it must be remembered that this is an abstraction to be complemented by self and final causation.

We inherit from our past, via the mode of efficient causation, the data for our physical, emotional and conceptual experience. We inherit, via this mode, data from our ecological and technical environments, our social-political environments, and our culture with its beliefs, values and ideals. All of these data which throb into our experience have an "actual" origin. The conceptual data or forms which are the defining forms or ideals are termed "eternal objects." Eternal objects will be discussed in detail later; the point to be made here is that we inherit via causal efficacy these conceptual "eternal objects" or conceptual forms, just as we do physical or material data. Whitehead states that the first phase of the mental pole of an emerging occasion is simply conceptual reproduction (PR 380-81).

> From each physical feeling there is the deri-
> vation of a purely conceptual feeling whose

datum is the eternal object exemplified in the definiteness of the actual entity, or the nexus, physically felt. . . . The mental pole starts with the conceptual registration of the physical pole [PR 379].[17]

We can say that just as our past and its material existence throbs into our existence with vector force, so do the forms of our material and social existence, and the conceptual beliefs, forms, or ideals of our cultural past. While both "eternal objects" and culture are abstractions which can have some "real" existence without their physical counterpart, they can have no "actual" existence without actualization in the material world. For example racial equality before the law has some real existence as a concept, but to be actual it must be manifested practically as well. What is important here is to understand that the one mode of causation, referred to as efficient causation, is not simply equated with material causation, but is understood as the mode by which data of our past, both conceptual and physical, "bring forth" the present with vector force.[18]

Whitehead most often speaks of eternal objects in terms of being determinant of the subject via the mode of final causation, partially because all eternal objects do not originate for the subject's experience from the past, but primarily because eternal objects provide the luring ideals which a subject chooses to define itself for itself and for the future. But the eternal objects which are determinant of present subjects were very often the same eternal objects which were determinant of the subjects which preceded the present, and which now provide the data for present subjects. In this way there is "conformation of the immediate present to the past [PR 364]," on both the physical and conceptual planes. This is what Whitehead is concerned with when he writes:

> There are eternal objects determinant of the definiteness of the objective datum which is the 'cause,' and eternal objects determinant of the definiteness of the subjective form belonging to the 'effect.' When there is reenaction there is one eternal object with two-way functioning, namely, as partial determinant of the objective datum, and as partial determinant of the subjective form. In this two-way role, the eternal object is functioning relationally between the initial data on the one hand and the concrescent subject on the other [PR 364].

20

Our material and conceptual past comes throbbing into our experience via the mode of efficient causation, and thus we gain most of the data for our subjective, physical and conceptual experience, and much of the data for our consciousness. To the extent that we are conscious of the primary feelings, prehensions, and perceptions (physical and conceptual), to that extent we can be conscious of "efficient causation."[19] In his discussion of the hand touching the stone, Whitehead speaks to this point.

> For example, in touch there is reference to the stone in contact with the hand, and a reference to the hand; but in normal, healthy, bodily operations the chain of occasions along the arm sinks into the background, almost into complete oblivion. Thus M̲, which has some analytic consciousness of its datum, is conscious of the feeling in its hand as the hand touches the stone. According to this account, perception in its primary form is consciousness of the causal efficacy of the external world by reason of which the percipient is a concrescence from a definitely constituted datum. The vector character of the datum is this causal efficacy.
>
> Thus perception, in this primary sense, is perception of the settled world in the past as constituted by its feeling-tones, and as efficacious by reason of those feeling-tones [PR 184].

I will discuss consciousness as a higher phase of concrescence below, but it is important here to note that consciousness of efficient causation is consciousness of a direct perception or inherited feeling-tone and by generalization, consciousness of the fact that we are who we are, in part, because we are "a concrescence from a definitely constituted datum," that datum being the "settled world in the past [PR 184]."

If we become conscious of the fact that we are who we are partially because of the causal efficacy of our settled past, and we are conscious of the fact that we inherit both material and conceptual, or environmental and cultural, data from our settled past then we can understand the conformity which we carry from our past as well as the fact that others around us, who share a nearly common environmental and cultural settled past, have significant conformity with us. It is this understanding

21

which enables Whitehead (as well as some social theorists) to speak of the social nature of reality including nature and persons. That is to say, all of reality is internally as well as externally related in some time in the historic process. And it follows from this understanding that, via inductive reasoning and generalization, statistically probable predictions can be made as to the character of actual entities and persons in the present and in the future by virtue of knowing something about their causal past.[20] This is true because the settled world as the environment for these actual entities and persons is the "ultimate ground" and "given fact" from which the emergent actual entities and persons come (PR 305-9).

> Every actual entity is in its nature essentially social; and this in two ways. First, the outlines of its own character are determined by the data which its environment provides for its process of feeling. Secondly, these data are not extrinsic to the entity; they constitute that display of the universe which is inherent in the entity. Thus the data upon which the subject passes judgment are themselves components conditioning the character of the judging subject. It follows that any general presupposition as to the character of the experiencing subject also implies a general presupposition as to the social environment providing the display for that subject [PR 309].

> It [induction] is the derivation of some characteristics of a particular future from the known characteristics of a particular past . . . . It is evident that, in this discussion of induction, the philosophy of organism appears as an enlargement of the premise in ethical discussions: that man is a social animal . . . . Another way of stating this explanation of the validity of induction is, that in every forecast there is a presupposition of a certain type of actual entities, and that the question then asked is, Under what circumstances will these entities find themselves? The reason that an answer can be given is that the presupposed type of entities requires a presupposed type of data for the primary phases of these actual entities; and that a presupposed type of data requires a presupposed type of social environment [PR 310-11].

The social environment in the above quotation is otherwise referred to as the settled past or determinant stubborn fact. Efficient causation is the mode by which this social environment becomes the inherent data for the initial phases of emergent actual entities and persons. This is our pre-determined nature, and consciousness of this origin of ourselves would be futile knowledge were it not for the abstract modes of self and final causation. Consciousness of our social nature and of the mode of efficient causation (in telling us that a "presupposed type of entities requires a presupposed type of data for the primary phase of the actual entities") tells us that if we want to be a certain type of person, or persons with certain types of experiences, this will require a certain type of social environment to be the relevant past environment of those experiences.[21]

The question then asked is, how can a person intervene in this causal process to create the requisite social environment for the desired type of future persons? The possible answer will become clearer after I have examined self-causation and final causation.

4. Consciousness in Relation to
Final Causation, i.e., Eternal
Objects or Ideal Possibilities

Eternal objects are "Pure Potentials for the Specific Determination of Fact, or Forms of Definiteness [PR 32]." Eternal objects for Whitehead are analogous to Platonic forms; they are the unchanging forms which give definite shape to actual occasions, that is to say, ". . . in respect of each actual entity, there is givenness of such forms. The determinate definiteness of each actuality is an expression of a selection from these forms [PR 69]." For Whitehead it is not substance which is permanent but these forms or potentials (PR 44). These forms or potentials have the character of being real without being actual as their conceptual recognition does not necessarily involve a ". . . necessary reference to any definite actual entities of the temporal world [PR 70]." They achieve actuality only through their ingression in actual entities. Eternal objects can also be termed ideas so long as this use is not restricted to conscious mentality (PR 37).

According to Whitehead's ontological principle, everything comes from somewhere and everything must be somewhere. And for him there are no new or novel eternal objects. These two statements drive him to a derivative notion of God, because if the eternal objects are eternal and there are no novel eternal objects, from whence cometh new forms? They are with God. For Whitehead, God is the residence of those eternal objects which are not yet real and/or actual in the world. While this is true of eternal objects, as we shall see below, it is not true of novel complex propositions or conceptual forms. In our daily lives the primary source of ideas and conceptual feelings is via efficient causation from our environment and the secondary source is the mental subjective struggle with already real ideas and concepts. Whitehead writes: "Conceptual feelings are primarily derivate from physical feelings and secondarily from each other. In this statement, the consideration of God's intervention is excluded [PR 378]." That is to say, the primary source of conceptual forms, ideas and conceptual possibilities, for emerging actual occasions or persons, is from physical feelings of settled social environment via the mode of efficient causation. The feelings are the feelings of the present subject feeling the past physical and conceptual social environment.

Secondarily conceptual feelings, i.e., feelings of eternal objects, may come from each other. This is possible in the subjective phase of actual entities. For conscious persons this emergence of novel complex conceptual forms is the most obvious in the "negative judgment."22

> Consciousness is the feeling of negation: in the perception of 'the stone as grey,' such feeling is in barest germ; in the perception of 'the stone is not grey,' such feeling is full development. Thus the negative perception is the triumph of consciousness. It finally rises to the peak of free imagination, in which the conceptual novelties search through a universe in which they are not datively exemplified [PR 245].

We gain via causal efficacy the physical-conceptual feeling that the stone is grey. We experience in consciousness the judgment that the stone might not be grey, and then through "free imagination" we experience the conceptual possibility of a stone such as we have never experienced in actuality. The artists, philosophers, and architects of buildings, cities and societies have such novel complex conceptions, and by ingressing them into actual entities, they add these novel actual entities to the social environment of the future. It is thus possible for novel complex forms, possibilities and ideals to emerge from the ongoing process of history. While Whitehead does not affirm this for eternal objects he does for propositions or theories which are novel complex combinations of forms with reference to specific matter. These propositions may be potential, i.e., held in the mental pole of an actual occasion, or they may be actualized.

> Evidently new propositions come into being with the creative advance of the world. For every proposition involves its logical subjects; and it cannot be the proposition which it is, unless those logical subjects are the actual entities which they are. Thus no actual entity can feel a proposition, if its actual world does not include the logical subjects of that proposition [PR 396].

New "propositions" thus do not emerge except with reference to actual entities which are the logical subjects of the proposition. The last sentence of the above quotation must be read carefully; there is an important distinction between actual and logical. Novelty of proposition or theory is possible for a person to experience or create, but that proposition will always be logically grounded in that person's actual world. This is another way of saying that "every conceptual feeling has a physical basis," even though it may be new (PR 398).

> From each physical feeling there is the derivation of a purely conceptual feeling whose datum is the eternal object exemplified in the definiteness of the actual entity, or the nexus, physically felt.
> This category (of conceptual valuation) maintains the old principle that mentality originates from sensitive experience. It lays down the principle that all sensitive experience originates mental operations. It does not, however, mean that there is no origination of other mental operations derivative from these primary mental operations. Nor does it mean that these mental operations involve consciousness, which is the product of intricate integration [PR 379].

Propositions are not pure conceptual feelings, but this qualification does not invalidate the application of the

25

above quotation to the origin and development of propositions.

Eternal objects come to the emergent subject or person primarily from the social environment (PR 489), and some are created for itself by the subject through negative judgment and imagination. Their function for the subject is to be selected by the subject, to give the subject his/her form or shape. The eternal objects inherited from the social environment provide the same definiteness for the present as they did for the past: "When there is re-enaction there is one eternal object with two-way functioning, namely as partial determinant of the objective datum, and as partial determinant of the subjective form [PR 364]." In this way there is conformation and continuity between the past and the present.

The eternal objects which are the determinant forms for an emergent subject are also called an "ideal" for that subject.

> The determinate unity of an actual entity is bound together by the final causation towards an ideal progressively defined by its progressive relation to the determinations and indeterminations of the datum. The ideal itself felt, defines what 'self' shall arise from the datum; and the ideal is also an element in the self which thus arises [PR 228].

The ideal which is an element of the emergent person or subject, as its defining ideal, is itself felt. The subject feeling the past as it is inherited with vector force is termed efficient causation; so in parallel manner the subject feeling the luring of the potential future as defined in the selected ideals is called "final causation."[23] In each case the causation is internal, and in the former case the causation is also external. Together they are the push of the past and the pull of the future, felt internally by the experiencing subject.[24]

> The 'lure for feeling' is the final cause guiding the concrescence of feelings. By this concrescence the multifold datum of the primary phase is gathered into the unity of the final satisfaction of feeling [PR 281].

Similarly, if we refer to "propositions" or "theories," which are more complex forms of potentiality and which are experienced by more complex actual entities such as persons, we find Whitehead again affirming the notion of

26

final causation, that is to say, the proposition is not just there, but rather, in the context of a subject it is luring. "It is an essential doctrine in the philosophy of organism that the primary function of a proposition is to be relevant as a lure for feeling [PR 37]."

Eternal objects in their more complex forms are "propositions" or theories and as such are the content of conceptual or mental operations. According to Whitehead these complex mental operations may or may not occur in human consciousness. In any case, the propositions function as eternal objects and thus provide the person who is conscious of these propositions with conceptual notions of what is, what is not, and what might be, i.e., (i) what is possibly true as opposed to what is perceived, and (ii) what is possible for the present and future. They also function as the defining ideals for the person; in this case those that are dominant will be luring the individual toward a particular kind of experience, toward becoming a particular type of person, or toward doing a particular kind of action. In this way the propositions are valuative, that is to say, they (as inherently part of the person) will influence the person to include or exclude certain feelings or prehensions from this person's social environment.[25] An example of this valuational function of propositions is what is meant when we speak of persons holding beliefs or ideologies; or more accurately being held by those beliefs or ideologies.[26]

Conscious persons may at times also experience propositions in a more (but never entirely) neutral and intellectual sense, that is to say, consciousness can struggle with judgments concerning what is, what is not, and what might be, utilizing the propositions held in consciousness as the means of testing the pragmatic possibilities of particular syntheses of conceptual and physical combinations; these tests at one level to be done not in actuality but mentally, in terms of logical coherence and in light of what we can empirically, imaginatively and inductively conclude from and about our past history of experiences.[27] This leads logically to a more explicit discussion of consciousness as subject.

5. Consciousness in Relation to Self-Causation, i.e., to Subjective Aim

Between vector past and the luring future is the emergent, experiencing subject or person.[28] The character of reality, including persons, is social. The character of the emergent subject is also individual and

27

experiential.[29] The past has no efficient causation outside of the experience of emergent subjects, and the ideal possibilities or eternal objects have no luring appeal outside the experience of the emergent subject.[30] The emergent individual subject has the capacity to influence (i) the character of his/her own experience, and (ii) the character of what he/she will become as a "superject" for the future.[31] This dual capacity is the capacity of self-causation (PR 228), and is termed the "subjective aim." "This subjective aim is this subject itself determining its own self-creation as one creature [PR 108]." Whitehead often does not use this language but rather speaks of the subject already having chosen its ideal for what it wants to be; this subject with its chosen ideal is termed "final causation" (PR 320 & 329). But the abstract distinction (of self-causation from final causation) does not violate his system of thought as long as we are clear that there is no self-causing subject without eternal objects or a past. This is demonstrated by the fact that Whitehead himself holds that the primary act of freedom on the part of a subject, for which the subject is responsible, is the selection of his/her ideals, which will give specificity and form to his/her concrescence.

> To be causa sui means that the process of concrescence is its own reason for the decision in respect to the qualitative clothing of feelings. It is finally responsible for the decision by which any lure for feeling is admitted to efficiency. The freedom inherent in the universe is constituted by this element of self-causation [PR 135, see also 380].

To be causa sui means that a person is finally one's own reason for the decision one makes with reference to choosing the ideals, beliefs and ideology, and also the physical factors, which make up and structure one's actual life. If there is freedom in the universe, it is found in these decisions.

Each individual subject is not only the locus of experience, but each individual is novel or unique. The novelty may not be great, but the experience of each subject is novel because one subjectively appropriates and responds to one's inherited environment in one's own way.[32] It never happened exactly this way before and never will again; it is primarily due to the fact that no other subjective moment, even in the subject's historic route of experiences, will ever be at the same relative place in time, that is to say, will ever have the same past.

It is in this process or moment of self-causation of
novelty (of deciding on one's defining ideals, of deciding
what of one's inheritance one will accept and appropriate)
that creativity enters the world;[33] not only for the
subject, but for the future, because the character which
one actualizes in one's life will be the character which
one becomes for others, and one's future experiences in
the future. Whitehead says it this way:

> The world is self-creative; and the actual
> entity as self-creating creature passes into
> its immortal function of part-creator of the
> transcendant world. In its self-creation the
> actual entity is guided by its ideal of itself
> as individual satisfaction and as transcendant
> creator [PR 130].

For Whitehead the creative process is rhythmic, that
is to say, it swings from the "publicity of many things"
in the social environment to the "individual privacy" of
the individual person; and it swings back from the private
individual to the publicity of the objectified individual
who has now become a datum in the social environment.[34]
"The former swing is dominated by the final cause, which
is the ideal; and the latter swing is dominated by the
efficient cause which is actual [PR 229]." In the midst
of this process there are moments of experience, and
moments of decision.

It is these decisions which must be made consciously if persons are to intervene consciously in the ongoing
process of history. Consciousness is, for Whitehead, "the
crown of experience, only occasionally attained, not its
necessary base [PR 408]." Consciousness is the highest
(not primary) phase of the category of subjective aim; and
as such is nothing more than subjective aim; that is to
say, the subjective aim of a person, conscious or not,
still operates between the vector inheritance of his/her
social environment and the luring force of ideals. When
consciouness emerges, as a conscious person one finds one-
self already an heir (novel but nonetheless an heir) of
one's social environment and past. And one probably also
finds one-self already held by the luring force of specific defining ideals or beliefs, which one has chosen pre-
consciously or unconsciously because they too were inherited with vector force from the past and social environment. At the moment of conscious experience, persons
are already late in the development of that present
experience; it is well formed by the forces of efficient
causation, final causation, and pre-conscious subjective

decisions.[35] Nonetheless subjective aim at the conscious
level does, according to Whitehead, have unique possibilities for conscious understanding of, and intervention
in, the process of human history, and this is due to the
capacity to have intellectual feelings.[36] What is an
intellectual feeling? "In an intellectual feeling the
datum is the generic contrast between a nexus of actual
entities and a proposition with its logical subjects
members of the nexus [PR 407]." Or more simply it is
feeling "the contrast between 'in fact' and 'might be' in
respect to particular instances in this actual world [PR
407]." It is the emergence of this capacity at the point
between social heritage, and the potentiality of the
present and the future, which brings us to the second
section of this chapter.

B. Consciousness at the Point between Social Heritage and Real Possibility

1. The Capacity to Make Negative Judgments

Whitehead in Process and Reality first introduces
the notion of "negative judgment" when he is only four
pages into the text. He writes that the "negative judgment is the peak of mentality [PR 7]." He makes this
statement in the midst of his discussion on "speculative
philosophy," which is the method which he purports to use
and which is thus both cause (method) and result of his
study, that is to say, this method is how he arrives at his
philosophy, and it is also the natural method of conscious
intelligence within the scheme of his philosophy.[37]

Whitehead states that to the empirical inductive
method[38] must be added "the play of a free imagination,
controlled by the requirements of coherence and logic [PR
7]." One must begin, he says, with the "ground of
particular observation," that is to say, with the observation of the stubborn facts of the social environment,
i.e., that which is there and related to us via efficient
causation and (as I will discuss below) presentational
immediacy. One then "makes a flight in the thin air of
imaginative generalization [PR 7]." The reason for adding
imaginative generalization is to explore consciously what
might be. At this point in his discussion the might be are
"factors which are consistently present," but not observed by empirical methods, but which may be "observed
under the influence of imaginative thought" which "sup-
plies the differences which the direct observation
lacks." After the flight of imaginative generalization

one "again lands for renewed observation rendered acute by rational interpretation."[39] This method enables a person to gain clarity as to the what and the how of our social environment and our becoming.[40]

Whitehead's concern here is with "consistency," i.e., with what might be, in fact, if our perceptions and generalizations are true. But this method can also "play with inconsistency" or with the might be of what is not, but is possible, for the present and/or future. This second kind of effort would ". . . throw light on the consistent, and persistent, elements in experience by comparison with what in imagination is inconsistent with them [PR 7]." This judgment of what something is not, by comparing it in our conscious imagination with that which is inconsistent or different from it (e.g., "the stone is not grey") is the negative judgment, which is the peak of mentality. It is this because it is a judgment of (i) what is in fact, (ii) what is not, and (iii) what might be. "It is the feeling of absence, and it feels this absence as produced by the definite exclusiveness of what is really present [PR 417]."

The negative judgment is a means of illustrating an alternative from what is in fact.[41]

> The general case of conscious perception is the negative perception, namely, 'perceiving this stone as not grey.' The 'grey' then has ingression in its full character of a conceptual novelty, illustrating an alternative [PR 245].

This is an example of consciousness functioning between social heritage and real possibility, because it is a judgment about this stone, i.e., an actual stone and a real alternative for the future occasions of the stone's duration, e.g., we might paint the stone grey.[42]

Let us make the judgment more complex and directly applicable to social theory, and say, "the children of Boston do not have access to free medical care." This is a negative judgment because it is generalized from particular facts within a particular social environment, and it gives rise to the alternative, inconsistent proposition, "the children of Boston do have access to free medical care." This is a "non-conformal proposition [PR 284]," because it is not a conformation of intellectual feeling with fact. In its purely logical aspect it is "merely wrong." But what happens is that "[w]hen a non-conformal proposition is admitted into feeling, the reaction to the datum has resulted in the synthesis of fact with alternative potentiality of the complex predicate. A novelty has emerged into creation [PR 284]." This novelty is conceptual; it is a new form, "or at least an old form in a new function" which has been introduced into the actual world by the conscious subject. It is easy enough to see here the primary categories of the process; (i) the social environment, i.e., actual children, in an actual situation actualizing a particular ideal or form in their relationship to a particular factor (medical care) in their social environment, and (ii) the eternal object or form, i.e., the non-conformal proposition which was introduced into the actual world by (iii) the conscious subject, i.e., the subjective aim.

It is the high point of consciousness to make negative judgments, and it is essential for persons who wish to intervene consciously in the process of their history to perceive what is, and from the exclusiveness of what is really present to feel and perceive absence, i.e., what is not, and finally to continue from these two to conceptions of what might be.[43] This process is the necessary first step toward conscious, active intervention in the process of history,[44] but it must be followed with more elaborate theories (including analyses and goals) which accurately describe what is in such a way as to give the subject maximum power to shape the future.

2. The Capacity to Theorize for the Purpose of Intervening in the Process of History

The primary category here is proposition,[45] sometimes equated with theory (PR 280), and very close to the term hypothesis (PR 309ff).

> A proposition is a new kind of entity. It is a hybrid between pure potentialities and actualities. A 'singular' proposition is the potentiality of an actual world including a definite set of actual entities in a nexus of reactions involving the hypothetical ingression of a definite set of eternal objects [PR 282].

According to this definition, the non-conformal proposition: "children in Boston do have access to free medical care," is a proposition because it is a potentiality for an actual world, that is to say, it is a real potentiality for the actual children of Boston, who are in a nexus of reactions involving the "hypothetical ingressing of a definite set of eternal objects," i.e., a definite set of formal relations, i.e., receiving free medical care. In the above definition the "definite set of actual entities" (in this case the children) are called the "logical subjects of the proposition" and the definite set of eternal objects involved (in this case the potential formal relations) are called the "predicates of the proposition." This is one of the few senses in which Whitehead uses "subject-predicate" language. But the situation warrants it because in actuality the children and the medical services are actual and are now in an actual set of formal relations; if there is to be the change proposed in the non-conformal proposition, they will be the subjects of that change which is predicated by the form changes as determined by the set of eternal objects in the non-conformal proposition. The proposition is a complex of determinate actual entities and persons, partially abstracted from their defining eternal objects (formal relations), and new eternal objects or formal relations, created by a subject by means of the capacity to make negative judgments (PR 392-93). In this sense the conceptual feeling of the conscious person created the predicative pattern, and "the logical subjects are reduced to the status of food for a possibility [PR 394]."

The proposition is not a general theory but "is the possibility of that predicate applying in that assigned way to those logical subjects [PR 394]." Nonetheless for this kind of specific proposition to be trusted as a real possibility it presupposes a perception of the actual situation that is accurate, and general theoretical knowledge of how the process, of moving from what is to what might be, works. There must be specific knowledge of the what and general knowledge of the how.

Process and Reality is an attempt through the method of "speculative philosophy" (PR 7-8), to provide general knowledge of the how of the process, as well as general knowledge of the what, i.e., knowledge which pertains to all facts. The character of the how and the general what, are explained in the principle of process: the being of an actual entity is constituted by its becoming (PR 34-35). For our purpose we can say that all actuality, past, present, and future, is caused, via the modes of efficient, final and self-causation (and is thus social in nature), and that in this process, a conscious, subjective person, at times, has the capacity (i) to understand the what of the past, by means of "speculative philosophy" and

33

inductive generalization,[46] (ii) to understand the general character of becoming, (iii) to make negative judgments, and (iv) consciously to create novel, non-conformal (as well as conformal) propositions and thus to illustrate alternatives, from the past, for the present and the future.

In order for persons to intervene consciously and effectively in the process of history, and to give their present and future the content and form which they choose, they must acknowledge their social origins and the modes of causation.[47] In fact it is precisely by using this knowledge that intervention can be most effectively achieved. Conscious intervention will thus include these phases: First we gain understanding of our past and contemporary present through "speculative philosophy." Next we gain understanding[48] of the process by which history moves forward. Then we reason inductively[49] (from what we know of the past and the nature of the process) that if a certain type of actual occasion (e.g., a child paying for medical care), is dominant in the past and present, it is probable that it will be in the future unless the social environment is changed.[50] Finally, we make decisions, and by selective ingression and arrangement[51] of physical and conceptual data we create the type of person we will be for our present experience, and, as superject, for our future self and our future public.[52]

By generalization we can make these same decisions, for the larger society, of which we are an internally as well as externally related part, as it moves from occasion to occasion, moment to moment through the duration of its history. We begin by entertaining propositions which refer to the actual situation and which describe the type of person or social situation which we desire. The proposition must (i) accurately account for the dominant physical and conceptual data of the social environment, and (ii) the proposition must entertain alternative forms which it is possible compatibly to combine in actuality with the logical subjects,[53] and which when actualized will enable the desired experience, and become the type of entity which will provide the type of physical and conceptual environment which we desire for the future.

The test of the predictive truth of a proposition lies in the future, the test of the predicative capacity of a proposition lies in the pragmatic, and the test of the value of a proposition lies in the experience of future entities. There are conformal propositions which say, for example, ABC is what has been, is now and will be in the future, and non-conformal propositions which say, for example, ABC is what has been, and ABD has not been, but is now entertained as a possibility and as an ideal for what will be in the future. The predictive truth of either proposition can be judged only in the future (PR 290-291). The test of the predicative capacity of the non-conformal proposition will also come in the future but the focus will be on the efficiency of the power of final causation exerted by the proposition[54] and whether or not in actuality the logical subjects of the proposition are as compatible with the predicate as they were when combined conceptually in the proposition, that is to say, is the actuality as workable as the theory?[55] Finally, also in the future, the value of the proposition, if actualized, will be the quality of experience of persons living out of that definite type of social environment.

> A judgment is a feeling in the 'process' of the judging subject, and it is correct or incorrect respecting <u>that</u> subject, . . . and it can only be criticized by the judgments of actual entities in the future [PR 291].

Over time a process of conscious intervention, actualization and testing can emerge;[56] such a process is sometimes called "theory and practice" or "praxis." Whitehead writes:

> The proper satisfaction to be derived from speculative thought is elucidation. It is for this reason that fact is supreme over thought. This supremacy is the basis of authority. We scan the world to find evidence for this elucidatory power.
> Thus the supreme verification of the speculative flight is that it issues in the establishment of a practical technique for well-attested ends, and the speculative system maintains itself as the elucidation of that technique. In this way there is the progress from thought to practice, and regress from practice to the same thought. This interplay of thought and practice is the supreme authority [FR 80-81].

Praxis is the highest level of a person's capacity to theorize for the purpose of intervening in the process of history because it is the active, conscious rehearsal of the process of (i) accounting for and acknowledging what is in fact, (ii) judging what is, what is not and what might be (this includes evaluation of our existence, including its decisions, theories and feelings), (iii) proposing what might be (this includes new theory building), (iv) choosing one's defining proposition (act of decision for particular belief or ideology), and (v) actualizing oneself and one's environment as nearly as possible according to that defining proposition.[57]

> When we survey the history of thought, and likewise the history of practice, we find that one idea after another is tried out, its limitations defined, and its core of truth elicited. . . . At the very least, men do what they can in the way of systematization, and in the event achieve something. The proper test is not that of finality, but of progress [PR 21].

According to Whitehead, we live in a causal world, and thus a predictable world, with the capacity to intervene consciously in history via proposition and concrescence, or theory and practice. We turn now to a discussion of our capacity to influence our present and future, and the public future.

3. The Capacity to Influence Our Present and the Future

"The mental operations have a double office. [First] they achieve, in the immediate subject, the subjective aim of that subject as to the satisfaction to be obtained from its own initial data [PR 423]." This is the office of influencing the present for the sake of the present experience. "In this way the decision derived from the actual world, which is the efficient cause, is completed by the decision embodied in the subjective aim which is the final cause [PR 423]." That is to say that a person influences his/her own present experience consciously or unconsciously, always in the context of past decisions which are embodied in the social environment which he/she inherits. Furthermore, since intellectual consciousness "only arises in a late derivative phase of complex integrations [PR 245]," and occurs very late in the concrescence of the actual occasion (i.e., the experience of the person), in which it occurs, it is confronted with itself (i.e., the moment of experience) being very nearly complete or actualized. In this late phase of any moment which is conscious, a person finds that most of the decisions for that moment have already been made (i) in the actual past social environment or the past occasions of his/her own life's duration, and which are now inherited with vector force, or (ii) in the earlier pre-conscious phases of the present experience.[58] In the first phase conceptual feelings are purely derivative from the past; this is termed "conceptual reproduction." In the second phase which also is pre-conscious, persons gain eternal objects by "conceptual reversion." Consciousness does not emerge until the third phase, i.e., "transmutation [PR 379-84]."[59] Not only does the conscious person find that most of the primary decisions already have been made for him/her, but he/she has only dim and select awareness of the early phases of the present (PR 22). Consciousness, according to Whitehead, "only dimly illuminates the prehensions in the mode of causal efficacy, because these prehensions are primitive elements in our experience [PR 246]." This is important because it explains why we do not have a clear conscious experience or feeling of the force of efficient causation in the creation of our experiences and our lives. We do not consciously feel caused! What we experience most vividly in our consciousness is the rich experience of making decisions and judgments of the conformal and non-conformal proposition types.[60] This is a sense of freedom and power, and it is both of these; but it is not nearly as significant an act of self-causation for the present experience as it seems to consciousness, because the conscious person has consciousness only of the highest phase of this experience and only dim consciousness of his/her efficiently caused phase. What we probably experience next most vividly in consciousness is the power (final cause) of the propositions, ideals or beliefs which we have chosen to guide the formation of selves. We experience the force of ideals when we are held by our beliefs. Thus to our conscious experience, our freedom to decide and the luring force of our ideals feel much more powerful than does our social environment which feels in consciousness as though it is just there. And so it should, because at the late conscious phase of an experience our social environment has done its work; we originated from it and we now embody it (PR 22). Efficient causation is essentially finished with respect to that experience when consciousness emerges, and thus consciousness can illuminate efficient causation only derivatively (PR 245-56).

By what mode then do we gain the clear images which we have in our consciousness of the world around us? We do so by the mode of presentational immediacy.[61] "Presentational immediacy is our perception of the contemporary world by means of the senses [PR 474]." Whitehead further explains presentational immediacy as follows:

> This type of experience is the lesson of the
> past reflected into the present. The more
> important contemporary occasions are those in
> the near neighbourhood. Their actual worlds
> are practically identical with that of the per-
> cipient subject. The percipient prehends the
> nexus of contemporary occasions by the media-
> tion of eternal objects which it inherits from
> its own past [PR 484-85].

The first part of this quotation is self explanatory, and
the last sentence simply means that, as a conscious
person, one perceives the public things, persons and
events around one, and orders them in one's mind according
to the conceptual understandings which one inherited from
one's own past. He continues: "Also it [the percipient]
selects the contemporary nexus thus prehended by the
efficacy of strains whose focal regions are important
elements in the past of those nexus [PR 485]." He means
by this that a person selects (i.e., discriminates between) public facts, which he perceives, by reference to
the traits which have been dominant and important in the
past of those public facts.[62] This can be something as
simple as (until recently) seeing a nurse rather than a
doctor when we saw a woman in uniform in a hospital.[63]
Whitehead concludes this passage on presentational immediacy this way:

> Thus, for successful organisms, presentational
> immediacy--though it yields no direct experi-
> ence about the contemporary world, and though
> in unfortunate instances the experience which
> it does yield may be irrelevant--does yield
> experience which expresses how the contempor-
> ary world has in fact emerged from its own past
> [PR 485].

Via presentational immediacy we learn empirical information which if complemented with "imagination, controlled
by the requirements of coherence and logic," can be
organized and generalized so as to yield "experience which
expresses how the contemporary world [including our-
selves] has in fact emerged from its own past [PR 485]."

Whitehead's statement that presentational immediacy
yields "no direct experience about the contemporary
world" means that there is not a direct reproduction
between what our senses experience and what our conscious
mind images. It does not mean that the rock is not actual
or that the experience that the rock is grey is not

statistically probably true. All it means is that con-scious awareness of contemporaries is a derived, not a direct experience.[64] "Perception is simply the cognition of prehensive unification; or more shortly, perception is cognition of prehension [SMW 71]."

I have included a discussion of presentational im-mediacy here because, while it is not directly causal, it is the primary mode by which our consciousness gains derivative information which enables the conscious person to understand his/her contemporary environment and pro-cess, and thus to be able to influence his/her present and the future. Experience gained via presentational imme-diacy comes, as we have said above, in a late phase of the experience, i.e., when the moment of experience is nearly formed. Thus while the experience gained via presenta-tional immediacy may be very significant for the level and content of that moment's personal satisfaction, the ex-perience so gained does not play a role in the primary formation of the experiencing occasion. This is true, because, as I said above, this occasion is already nearly complete. This is a subtle but very important point because it leads us to the conclusion that a conscious person has very little capacity to influence the content and form of the present experience since this experience is nearly complete before consciousness emerges.

To be a significant intentional influence, and to intervene consciously in the flow or process of history, a person must influence the late phase of the present in such a way that the present becomes the desired determi-nant past for the future.[65] This is the second of the "double office" of mental operations. In this second function we are concerned with "the relative efficiency of the various feelings to enter into the objectifications of that subject in the creative advance beyond itself [PR 423]."[66] This is the subject as superject, or what Whitehead sees as the third and last of an actual entity's three-fold character (PR 134). It is, as it were, what one makes of one-self out of the past and present, for the future. In one's early phase one is the inheritor of efficient cause; in one's last phase one is the data of efficient cause for the subjects of the future.

> An actual entity considered in reference to the publicity of things is a 'superject;' namely, it arises from the publicity which it finds, and adds itself to the publicity which it transmits. It is a moment of passage from decided public facts to a novel public fact [PR 443].

It is toward this capacity as a novel public fact with the capacity of efficient causation for the future that a person must focus if he/she wishes consciously to intervene most effectively in history. It is in the late phase of concrescence that we can intervene by consciously including conceptual and physical data in that occasion and thus give it objective status for the future.[67] We thus have the capacity to intervene consciously in our present activity as transcendent creator[68] of the future physical-conceptual world.

> . . . the future has <u>objective</u> reality in the present, but no <u>formal</u> actuality. For it is inherent in the constitution of the immediate, present actuality that a future will supersede it. Also conditions to which that future must conform, including real relationships to the present, are really objective in the immediate actuality [PR 327].

Consider, for example, the decision and act of enrolling in college, joining the army, learning to drive, learning to read, or conceiving a child; in each case there is the subjective experience of that occasion but the greater significance is that all future occasions in the historic route of that person's life and the occasions of others' lives who will have direct or indirect contact with that person will be influenced by the vector inheritance of that one actualized experience. "An actual entity [or moment of experience] arises from decisions <u>for</u> it, and by its very existence provides decisions <u>for</u> other actual entities which supersede it [PR 68]." What we consciously include or exclude from any of our immediate experiences will be significant for the subjective enjoyment of that moment, but while the subjectivity of that moment will cease, that concrete moment will continue as effect. Thus if we want to intervene consciously and to give direction to history we will focus on the inheritance or effect of our moments, and upon the unfolding multitude of subjective feelings which will be effected; rather than focusing on the immediate enjoyment of the present experience.[69]

Having located the moment in the historic process wherein humans have the most freedom for making decisions for the future of themselves and their world, we have also located the moment of greatest ethical and moral responsibility.[70] Whitehead sees this clearly.

The greater part of morality hinges on the determination of relevance in the future. The relevant future consists of those elements in the anticipated future which are felt with effective intensity by the present subject by reason of the real potentiality for them to be derived from itself [PR 41].[71]

In the discussion thus far we have been analytical rather than normative, i.e., we have been concerned to understand the process in order to locate when and how persons can intervene consciously in history, and we have noted that this moment of greatest power for decision is therefore the locus of greatest moral responsibility, but we have not discussed what decisions would be good, nor what Whitehead means by progress, beyond an increase in subjective satisfaction. To this extent then the study and Whitehead's philosophy are descriptive rather than normative, scientific rather than ethical. This does not mean that every ethical system would be consonant with Whitehead's analysis, nor does it mean that Whitehead does not have an implicit and explicit ethics, or aesthetics, in his philosophy.[72] His ethics and aesthetics (which are considered by some to be essentially the same) have been systematically studied by others.[73]

For purposes of this study, we need to note only two general, but important, aspects of Whitehead's analysis which have normative implications for persons making actual decisions (and thus normative decisions, since all actual decisions are valuative) for the future. First, the nature of reality is social.[74] Second, the locus of experience is the individual.[75] For Whitehead, the locus of experience is by definition the locus of value, that is to say, the process is to be judged by the quality of experience it enables at the only point or time, in the process or in the universe, that there is an absolute reality and experience, viz., within the subjective moment.[76]

He writes:

. . . the element of value, of being valuable, of having value, of being an end in itself, of being something which is for its own sake, must not be omitted in any account of an event as the most concrete actual something. 'Value' is the word I use for the intrinsic reality of an event [SMW 93].

41

A subjective experience is more valuable as it increases in intensity and in harmony. And harmony of contrasts is more valuable than harmony of similarity. For example, note the human body; "The harmonized relations of the parts of the body constitute [its] wealth of inheritance into a harmony of contrasts, issuing into intensity of experience [PR 167]." Thus in this ontological scheme the definition of progress is the emergence or creation of a physical and conceptual environment which, via efficient and final causation, enhances intense, harmonious experience in individual subjects.[77]

The implication for social theory of these two statements (social nature of reality and experiential nature of subject), is the requirement of compatibility; that is to say, if a particular type of experience is desired for the subject, it must emerge from a compatible physical and conceptual social environment.[78] And specifically, if a person is intervening in the historical process by creating the type of environment which he/she hopes will bring forth a specific desired experience, then this person must first propose such a new environment in propositional form and then actualize it.[79] The proposition in this instance must be compatible with its logical subjects and with the desired experience.[80]

To understand further the requirement of compatibility we will discuss it as the last of four interrelated principles; (i) "ontological principle," (ii) "principle of relativity," (iii) "principle of intensive relevance," and (iv) "principle of compatibility and contrariety."

"Ontological principle:" The philosophy of organism (as we noted earlier) assumes that every actual entity is a composite unity of data primarily inherited from its social environment, which it shares in common to a significant extent, with its contemporaries; and that for anything to exist it must exist in some actual entity. Whitehead writes:

> It follows from the ontological principle, thus interpreted, that the notion of a 'common world' must find its exemplification in the constitution of each actual entity taken by itself for analysis. For an actual entity cannot be a member of a 'common world,' except in the sense that the 'common world' is a constituent of its own constitution [PR 224].

42

The ontological social nature of individuals is further clarified in the "principle of relativity," to which Whitehead refers as he continues the above quotation:

> It follows that every item of the universe, including all the actual entities, are constituents in the constitution of any one actual entity. This conclusion has already been employed under the title of the 'principle of relativity.' This principle of relativity is the axiom by which the ontological principle is rescued from issuing in an extreme monism [PR 224].

Individuals are individuals, but by the nature of their constitutions and the nature and origin of their becoming, they are internally as well as externally related to their external fellow individuals.[81]

The "principle of intensive relevance" explains how it is that these related, social individuals are not "undifferentiated repetitions, each of the other, with mere numerical diversity [PR 224]."

> The notion of intensive relevance is fundamental for the meaning of such concepts as 'alternative possibilities,' 'more or less,' 'important or negligible.' The principle asserts that any item of the universe, however preposterous as an abstract thought, or however remote as an actual entity, has its own gradation of relevance, as prehended, in the constitution of any one actual entity: it might have had more relevance; and it might have had less relevance, including the zero of relevance involved in the negative prehension; but in fact it has just that relevance whereby it finds its status in the constitution of that actual entity [PR 224].

The individual is a relative, composite unity of inherited and self-created items which participate in the individual's composition with greater or lesser degrees of relevance. If the individual is to experience unity, as well as compositeness, there must be some kind of compatibility between the items included in the composition of the individual, both by type and by degree of relevance.

43

There is interconnection between the degrees of relevance of different items in the same actual entity. This fact of interconnection is asserted in the 'principle of compatibility and contrariety.' There are items which, in certain respective gradations of relevance, are contraries to each other; so that those items, with their respective intensities of relevance, cannot co-exist in the constitution of one actual entity [PR 224-25].

From the above discussion, it follows that, if a praxis-oriented individual wished to intervene consciously in history in order to bring forth or facilitate a particular type of experience[82] among the individuals in his/her future or the future of the society involved, he/she would necessarily be concerned with the compatibility of the items which would go into making up propositional forms of these future occasions. In general theoretical terms, these items are (i) the physical, structural, and conceptual environment, (ii) the logical subjects, and (iii) the experiences desired or valued for those logical subjects. We can exemplify these items and the requirements of compatibility by referring again to the proposition; "the children in Boston have access to free health care," which we will term proposition "A".

If persons want to insure the experience of physical and mental health for all children in Boston, they at least will have to actualize a proposition which includes a set of formal relations[83] between the children and the health care delivery system, which guarantees all children access to adequate health care. This may or may not be proposition "A" but, learning from the history of health care delivery throughout the world, it is probable that proposition "A" is very close to a minimum (necessary if not sufficient) requirement. Thus we can speak of health requiring health care.

The desired experience of a child exercising free access to health care requires not only the logical subjects, i.e., children, and formal relations which structure and define that access, but also other compatible logical subjects, i.e., health care personnel and institutions, e.g., hospitals, who enter internally (conceptually and physically) into each child's experience of receiving that health care. This experience may be incompatible with certain types of experience by other subjects, i.e., if the children of Boston are to experience access to free health care, it will probably be

44

incompatible with the providers of that care experiencing the delivery of health care in terms of a freely negotiated financial contract for services rendered, that is to say, the socio-economic relations surrounding the delivery of health care would have to change and the implications of that are that the socio-economic relations (and experience) of the relative society would have to change since health care delivery would be economically supported by other than private sources.

Thus we have a brief example of the requirement for compatibility between particular types of experiences, the social environment out of which they emerge, and the experiencing subjects involved.

It follows logically then from the analysis in this chapter that while in one sense, an application of Whitehead's philosophy to social theory would be scientific, and ethically neutral, in another sense the social nature of individuals, and the "locus of experience in the individual," requires first, a social theory which is ontologically social in terms of (i) persons' relationships to persons, i.e., social, political, economic and cultural relations, (ii) persons' relationships to things and nature,[84] and (iii) aspects of nature in relation to other aspects of nature.[85] The latter two of these categories are now being championed by ecologists. Second, the application of Whitehead's philosophy would require the locus of the reference, for making valuational judgments in social planning, to be the subjective experience of individuals.

Whitehead's ethics have been discussed in other studies; and the implications of a social theory with this socialist-subjectivist analysis, for ethics, is a problem for another study. It is enough here to see that Whitehead's philosophy applied to social theory leads to a radically social (including ideas, man and nature) analysis combined with the value reference being the subjective experience of individuals.[86] And such a social theory will have force and appeal by virtue of the fact that it exemplifies the grandeur of the wider truth arising from the very nature of the order of things (AI 16).

C. Summary

Whitehead provides a systematic discussion and analysis of the nature of the on-going process of history, and by application, we gain the following notions which have pertinence for understanding the relationship of consciousness to existence, and the relationship of consciousness to the human capacity to intervene in history: (i) the ontological principle and the three modes of causality are fundamental categories of process, (ii) the nature of reality is thus social, and the locus of experience is the subjective individual, (iii) conscious information of our contemporary and historical world is possible via presentational immediacy, and knowledge of the nature of the causal, and thus predictable, process is possible when empirical research and imagination (controlled by coherence and logic) are aided by inductive reason and generalization, (iv) conscious persons have the capacity to make negative judgments, create and believe non-conformal propositions, and selectively include, exclude and arrange the physical and conceptual data of the late phases of their immediate experiences, and by so doing, (v) they can have some influence on their immediate subjective experience, and great influence on their relevant future, (vi) when making these decisions for the future, persons deal with the questions of compatibility of variables, and with value questions, i.e., what is desired for the subjective experience of individuals.

Specifying these categories and concepts is important because the main thrust of this chapter has been to explore the understanding of consciousness in the philosophy of organism in such a way as to identify and explicate these relevant categories and to facilitate the integration, or translation if necessary, of this understanding--and its categories and concepts--into language useful in Marxist theory. These categories, as summarized above, are the categories which I will bring to bear on problem areas in Marxist theory in Chapter III. In Chapter II and III I will make several references to these categories as I point up parallels between process philosophical categories, and categories and perspectives in Marxist theory; however, the primary purpose of Chapter II will be to discuss the relevant categories in Marxist theory as I have done with reference to process theory in this first chapter. And the primary purpose of Chapter III will be to explore the possible ways that the process categories discussed in this chapter may contribute to clarifying, by-passing and/or resolving relevant problems and unresolved issues in Marxist theory.

Chapter 1 - Notes

1. For a critical analysis of Whitehead's understanding of consciousness from a more "philosophical" perspective, see Donald Carl
Norris, "A Critique of Whitehead's Theory of Consciousness" (unpublished Ph.D. dissertation, Boston University, 1972).

2. William A. Christian, An Interpretation of Whitehead's Meta-
physics (New Haven: Yale University Press, 1967); Ivor Leclerc,
Whitehead's Metaphysics: An Introductory Exposition (London:
George Allen & Unwin, Ltd., 1958); Victor Lowe, Understanding
Whitehead (Baltimore: Johns Hopkins University Press, 1968), and
Donald W. Sherburne, A Key to Whitehead's Process and Reality (New
York: Macmillan Co., 1966).

3. The category of consciousness in Whitehead's philosophy has
been discussed in detail in other studies including Norris, "A
Critique of Whitehead's Theory of Consciousness;" and David A.
Crocker, "A Whiteheadian Theory of Intention and Actions," unpublished Ph.D. dissertation, Yale University, 1970. The focus of
the present study differs from the above, but their work will be
cited here when it is appropriate.

4. ". . . the immediate present has to conform to what the past is
for it, and the mere lapse of time is an abstraction from the more
concrete relatedness of 'conformation'. The 'substantial' character
of actual things is not primarily concerned with the prediction of
qualities. It expresses the stubborn fact that whatever is settled
and actual must in due measure be conformed to by the self-creative
activity. The phrase 'stubborn fact' exactly expresses the popular
apprehension of this characteristic." Alfred North Whitehead,
Symbolism (New York: Macmillan, 1927; Capricorn Books, 1959), pp.
36f & 37 hereafter referred to as SYM.

5. For a longer discussion of the ontological principle see William
A. Christian, "Whitehead's Explanation of the Past," in Alfred North
Whitehead: Essays on His Philosophy, ed. by George L. Kline
(Englewood Cliffs, N.J.: Prentice-Hall, 1963), pp. 93-99.

6. A usual qualification of this sentence is this:
"The ontological distinction between a human individual and a
society of such individuals is that implicit in the distinction
between a 'living' and a 'non-living' society. The difference
is that of the originative power of the individual and non-
originative character of the institutions and events of a social
complex abstracted from its individual members. That is, the
introduction of relevant novelty into the social complex is
accomplished only by the individual members. The institutions
of a society are embodiments of creative and novel expressions,
but are not, of themselves living, self-perpetuating struc-

tures." (David L. Hall, The Civilizations of Experience: A Whiteheadian Theory of Culture [New York: Fordham University Press, 1973], p. 68.)

This statement reflects a human vs. nature dualism more than it does Whitehead's understanding of what it means to be "alive" (PR 159-61).* It is in one sense true, i.e., moments in the duration of an institution probably do not experience subjective reactions or decisions to any greater extent than does a stone, however, (i) neither a human individual nor a social institution is originative when "abstracted from its individual members"; this is the fallacy of misplaced concreteness, (ii) institutions or things, once actualized, can be originative, e.g., steam power drove its respective civilization "away from inherited modes of order [AI 5]." This is not "living" but it is, via efficient causation, originative, and (iii) efficient causation means the power of self-perpetuation, again not in a "living" sense, but nonetheless, an actual sense.

The uniqueness of humans is not that they have the power to originate novelty or that they are alive, but as we will see in the present study, that they can originate novelty from a basis of conscious knowledge and reason,** and that they have personality:

"A tree is a democracy. Thus living bodies are not to be identified with living bodies under personal dominance. There is no necessary connection between 'life' and 'personality'. A 'personal' society need not be 'living', in the general sense of the term; and a 'living' society need not be 'personal' [AI 206]."

*See also Alfred North Whitehead, Adventures of Ideas (New York: Macmillan, 1933; Free Press, 1967), p. 207, hereafter referred to as AI.

**See also Alfred North Whitehead, The Function of Reason (Princeton: Princeton University Press, 1929; Boston, Beacon Press, 1958), p. 65, hereafter referred to as FR.

7.   Dalton D. Baldwin in "Evil and Persuasive Power: A Response to Hare and Madden," Process Studies, V3, N4 (Winter, 1973), p. 260, discusses efficient causation as determinism; final causation as persuasive power; and subjective aim as freedom.

8.   For a systematic analysis of actual occasions, see Johnson, Whitehead's Theory of Reality, pp. 16-57.

9.   "For Whitehead it is the influence of a world that is there for perception, stubborn fact not to be avoided, the ground from which the experient occasion must arise, the elements that must be taken into account. It is the iron hand of the given. The causal efficiency of the object, therefore, is its character of givenness exacting conformity." (Sheilah O'Flynn Brennan, "Perception and Causality: Whitehead and Aristotle," Process Studies, V3, N4 [Winter, 1973], p. 281.)

10. "Ideas, great men, economic activities, technological devices, the facts of 'geography,'--all influence the behavior of human beings." Johnson, Whitehead's Philosophy of Civilization, p. 22.

11. ". . . the actual entities which in 'passing' provide data, have a drive or urge to make contributions to new actual entities. Thus in this sense, data are not passively available." Johnson, Whitehead's Theory of Reality, p. 30.

12. Baldwin, in "Evil and Persuasive Power," also understands efficient causation in these terms; see especially pp. 259-283.

13. See below, pp. 19f., 22-25, 27f., 29, and 31ff.

14. In the context of the determinism-libertarianism debate, a good Whiteheadian critique of mechanistic determinism can be found in Edward Ira Stevens, "Freedom, Determinism, and Responsibility: An Analysis and a Whiteheadian Interpretation" (unpublished Ph.D. dissertation, Vanderbilt University, 1965). This is, however, something of a misplaced debate, in a cosmological system which includes and affirms the fundamentals of both determinism and freedom.

15. This notion is developed by Whitehead in his doctrines of Immanent Law and Internal Relations.
  "By the doctrine of Law as immanent it is meant that the order of nature expresses the characters of the real things which jointly compose the existences to be found in nature. When we understand the essences of these things, we thereby know their mutual relations to each other [AI 111-12]."
  ". . . a reason can now be produced why we should put some limited trust in induction. For if we assume an environment largely composed of a sort of existences whose natures we partly understand, then we have some knowledge of the laws of nature dominating that environment. But apart from that premise and apart from the doctrine of Immanent Law, we have no knowledge of the future. We should then acknowledge blank ignorance, and not make pretences about probability.
  ". . . the doctrine of Immanent Law is untenable unless we can construct a plausible metaphysical doctrine according to which the characters of the relevant things in nature are the outcome of their interconnections, and their interconnections are the outcome of their characters. This involves some doctrine of Internal Relations [AI 112-13]."

See also Alfred North Whitehead, Science and the Modern World (New York: Macmillan, 1925; Free Press, 1967), p. 152, hereafter referred to as SMW.

16. See also Baldwin, "Evil and Persuasive Power," p. 268; Johnson, Whitehead's Theory and Reality, pp. 13ff; and SMW, pp. 17, 36, 42 and 79.

17. "What happens in the second phase [viz., conceptual reversion (PR 380-81)] of concrescence is that the eternal objects, bedded fast in the concreteness of exclusive determination of a particular actual entity in the conformal phase, are pried loose, or abstracted from, that determinateness and become, as objects for the conceptual feeling, transcendent." (Donald W. Sherburne, A Whiteheadian Aesthetic [Hamden, Conn.: Archon Books, 1970], p. 50).

18. Baldwin in "Evil and Persuasive Power," pp. 259-60, and Ronald L. DuBois in "Reason in Ethics: A Whiteheadian Perspective" (unpublished Ph.D. dissertation, St. Louis University, 1971), p. 163, both fail to make this point, and they equate the coercive power of the physical world with efficient causation, and the ideal aim only with final causation. Ms. Brennan in "Perception and Causality," p. 277, however, makes the point when she says that what Whitehead is telling us is that "it is through the causal influence of the external world that form is received, . . ."

19. Perception, consequently, is ultimately rooted in causation." Brennan, "Perception and Causality," p. 227.

20. "Scientific study is able to present statistical information about what may be expected from the determined action of efficient cause." Baldwin, "Evil and Persuasive Power," p. 226; see also pp. 260 & 262.

21. As Baldwin points out in "Evil and Persuasive Power," p. 261, efficient causation is important for human purpose because it "provides for dependable generalizations which may guide human purpose, and furnishes a matrix of relativity in which the purpose may be expressed."

22. See also Sherburne, A Key to Whitehead's Process and Reality, pp. 207, 214 & 215.

23. The "subject" of Whitehead's Adventures of Ideas is the "general ideas" and the "highly specialized notions," i.e., the "intellectual agencies involved in the modification of epochs [AI 12]." In this sense it is a study in the history of culture but not an inclusive sociological analysis of the process of human history.

24. "Whitehead refers to men as being 'driven by their thoughts as well as by the molecules in their bodies, by intelligence and by senseless forces' [AI 58]. He mentions the 'compulsion of the truth' [AI 86] and describes the 'potentialities' in the final cause as 'dictating the form of composition which produce the issue' [MT* 128 f]." (Baldwin, "Evil and Persuasive Power," p. 262).

*MT here refers to Alfred North Whitehead, Modes of Thought, (New York: Macmillan Company, 1938), hereafter referred to as MT.

25.   "'As we think, we live.' [MT 87] The ideas we accept, as guiding principles, determine what we experience and what is barred from experience." Johnson, Whitehead's Philosophy of Civilization, p. 22.

26. For a discussion of the distinction between holding and being held by beliefs, see Clifford Geertz, Islam Observed (New Haven: Yale University, 1968; Chicago: Phoenix Books, 1971), pp. 16-19.

27. "[Philosophy] is a survey of possibilities and their comparison with actualities. In philosophy, the fact, the theory, the alternatives, and the ideal, are weighed together. Its gifts are insight and foresight, and a sense of the worth of life, in short, that sense of importance which nerves all civilized effort. . . .
    Every epoch has its character determined by the way its populations re-act to the material events which they encounter. This reaction is determined by their basic beliefs--by their hopes, their fears, their judgments of what is worth while. . . . Philosophy is an attempt to clarify those fundamental beliefs which finally determine the emphasis of attention that lies at the base of character [AI 98-99]."

28. For a more extensive discussion of subjective aim as it emerges between the past and the future, see Crocker, "A Whiteheadian Theory of Intentions and Actions," pp. 30-92.

29.   "The whole concept of absolute individuals with absolute rights, and with a contractual power of forming fully defined external relations, has broken down.   The human being is inseparable from its environment in each occasion of its existence.   The environment which the occasion inherits is immanent in it, and conversely it is immanent in the environment which it helps to transmit. . . . On the other hand, the inherited status is never a full determination. There is always the freedom for the determination of individual emphasis [AI 63]."

30. This is an important sentence; for a full discussion, see "Past, Present, Future," (AI 191-200).

31. "What is objective in the present is the necessity of a future of actual occasions, and the necessity that these future occasions conform to the conditions inherent in the essence of the present occasion [AI 195]."

32. "We are different from it, [the past] and yet we retain our individual identity with it. This is the mystery of personal identity, the mystery of the immanence of the past in the present, the mystery of transcience. All our science, all our explanations require concepts originating in this experience of derivation [AI 163-64]."

33. See Sherburne, A Key to Whitehead's Process and Reality, p. 218.

34. The rhythmic swing between causing and being caused is for Whitehead the nature of being. To cause is to have power over oneself and others. To be caused means that others have power over us. Here, Whitehead follows Plato: "Plato says that it is the definition of being that it exert power and be subject to the exertion of power [AI 120]." "It was Plato in his later mood who put forward the suggestion, 'and I hold that the definition of being is simply power.' This suggestion is the charter of the doctrine of Immanent Law [AI 129]."

35. Stevens, in "Freedom, Determinism, and Responsibility," p. 213, presents a view of the self as composed of both a "character-as-so-far-formed", and the power of making choices, seemingly, in spite of the influences of this character-as-so-far-formed and the environment. "Whitehead's cosmology," he writes, "provides a metaphysical ground for seeing man as influenced by his past, yet not determined by it, and thus as possessing freedom of choice, [sufficient for responsibility]." The task of the present study is to discuss the 'how' and 'when' a person's freedom can be exercised, not in spite of determinism, but within the ongoing causal process of history.

36. For a complementing discussion of (i) intellectual feelings, as feelings of propositions and (ii) consciousness of intention, see Crocker, "A Whiteheadian Theory of Intentions and Actions," pp. 198ff.

37. For a more extensive discussion, see "Philosophical Method" (AI 220-38).

38. On the inductive method Whitehead writes:
"We must observe the immediate occasion, and use reason to elicit a general description of its nature. Induction presupposes metaphysics. In other words, it rests upon an antecedent rationalism. You cannot have a rational justification for your appeal to history till your metaphysics has assured you that there is a history to appeal to; and likewise your conjectures as to the future presuppose some basis of knowledge that there is a future already subjected to some determinations. The difficulty is to make sense of either of these ideas. But unless you have done so, you have made nonsense of induction [SMW 44]."

39. "Theories are built upon facts; and conversely the reports upon facts are shot through and through with theoretical interpretation [AI 3]."

40. See also Johnson, Whitehead's Theory of Reality, pp. 7ff.

41. ". . . every actual occasion is set within a realm of alternative interconnected entities. This realm is disclosed by all the untrue propositions which can be predicated significantly of that occasion. It is the realm of alternative suggestions, whose foothold in actuality transcends each actual occasion [SMW 158]."

42. "It is simply descriptive of our experience that novel objective alternatives are entertained, . . ." DuBois, "Reason in Ethics," p. 180.

43. "It [individual perception] may represent the faintest ripple differentiating the general substrate energy; or, in the other extreme, it may rise to conscious thought, which includes poising before self-conscious judgment the abstract possibilities of value inherent in various situations of ideal togetherness [SMW 106]."

44. Crucial to Whitehead's historical vision is "the emancipation of social life through human self-awareness and application of creative intelligence to the control of activities." William M. Sullivan, "The Process Social Paradigm and the Problem of Social Order" (unpublished Ph.D. dissertation, Fordham University, 1971), p. 5.

45. For a full "scholastic" discussion of Whitehead's category of propositions, see Michael Louis Harrington, "Whitehead's Theory of Propositions" (unpublished Ph.D. dissertation, Emory University, 1973), especially pp. 146-172.

46. It is through an appeal to history and reason that we can understand not only the what of past, but the how of our becoming.

"The appeal to history is the appeal to summits of attainment beyond any immediate clarity in our own individual existence. It is an appeal to authority. The appeal to reason is the appeal to that ultimate judge, universal and yet individual to each, to which all authority must bow. History has authority so far, and exactly so far, as it admits of some measure of rational interpretation [AI 162]."

47. This is consonant with the rational systems model which "makes the fundamental assumption that the universe can be molded in desired directions by the conscious manipulation of specified 'causes' in order to create particular kinds of effects." Frances Elizabeth Svensson, "The Concept of Change: Alternative Perspectives" (unpublished Ph.D. dissertation, University of Washington, 1970), p. 98.

48. "To a large extent, understanding can be acquired by a conscious effort and it can be taught. Thus the training of Foresight is by the medium of Understanding. Foresight is the product of Insight. . . . The general topic to be understood is the entire internal functioning of human society, including its technologies, the biological and physical laws on which these technologies depend, and including the sociological reactions of humans depending on fundamental psychological principles. In fact, the general topic is sociology in the broadest sense of the term, including its auxiliary sciences [AI 89]."

49. "Creativity is unmistakably involved in the process of inductive thinking." Johnson, Whitehead's Theory of Reality, p. 89, see also all pp. 89-90.

50. ". . . the presupposed type of entities requires a presupposed type of data for the primary phases of these actual entities; and a presupposed type of data requires a presupposed type of social environment. But the laws of nature are the outcome of the social environment. Hence when we have presupposed a type of actual occasions, we have already some information as to the laws of nature in operation throughout the environment [PR 311]."

"Foresight. We require such an understanding of the present conditions, as may give us some grasp of the novelty which is about to produce a measurable influence on the immediate future. Yet the doctrine, that routine is dominant in any society that is not collapsing, must never be lost sight of. Thus the grounds, in human nature and in the successful satisfaction of purpose, these grounds for the current routine must be under-

54

stood; and at the same time the sorts of novelty just entering into social effectiveness have got to be weighed against the old routine. In this way the type of modification and the type of persistence exhibited in the immediate future may be foreseen [AI 93]."

51. ". . . clearly the way the past is disposed of is of crucial importance to the way in which it will be able to participate in the activity of the present and future." Svensson, "The Concept of Change," p. 152.

52. Whitehead, in Adventures of Ideas, p. 31, discusses the notion that every action is at once a private experience and a public utility.

53. "There are items which, in certain respective gradations of relevance, are contraries to each other; so that those items, with their respective intensities of relevance, cannot coexist in the constitution of one actual entity [PR 225]." See also PR 224-225 & 290.

54. "The ideals cherished in the souls of men enter into the character of their actions. These interactions within society modify the social laws by modifying the occasions to which those laws apply. Impracticable ideals are a program for reform. Such a program is not to be criticized by immediate possibilities. Progress consists in modifying the laws of nature so that the Republic on Earth may conform to that Society to be discerned ideally by the divination of Wisdom [AI 42]."

55. "The truth of a proposition lies in its truth-relation to the nexus which is its logical subject. A proposition is true when the nexus does in reality exemplify the pattern which is the predicate of the proposition [AI 244]."

56. ". . . empirically the development of self-justifying thoughts has been achieved by the complex process of generalizing from particular topics, of imaginatively schematizing the generalizations, and finally by renewed comparison of the imagined scheme with the direct experience to which it should apply [PR 24-25]."

57. Hall, in The Civilization of Experience, pp. 66ff, clearly delineates the locus and limits of freedom within a single occasion of human experience, but does not combine it with process to show the real significance of human freedom, which is for the future, through praxis.

58. "Our consciousness does not initiate our modes of functioning. We awake to find ourselves engaged in process, immersed in

satisfactions and dissatisfactions, and actively modifying, either by intensification, or by attenuation, or by the introduction of novel purposes. This primary procedure which is presupposed in consciousness, I will term Instinct. It is the mode of experience directly arising out of the urge of inheritance, individual and environmental [AI 46]."

59. "By means of transmutation, rocks, trees, people, etc., emerge as distinct entities from the welter of multitudinous microcosmic actual occasions. But these entities which emerge as a result of transmutation are abstractions from full concreteness of their component actual occasions; to treat these derivative entities as metaphysically ultimate is to commit the fallacy of misplaced concreteness." (Sherburne, A Whiteheadian Aesthetic, p. 59).

60. "Spontaneity, originality of decision, belongs to the essence of each actual occasion. It is the supreme expression of individuality: its conformal subjective form is the freedom of enjoyment derived from the enjoyment of freedom [AI 258]."

61. See also Sherburne, A Key to Whitehead's Process and Reality, pp. 214-15.

62. "In its metaphysical analysis 'order' is constituted by the dominance of some sets of characteristics in a group of nexus of actual entities. In other words, 'order' exists to the extent to which certain characteristics dominate." Leclerc, Whitehead's Metaphysics, p. 214.

63. For further discussion of this issue, see Brennan, "Perception and Causality," pp. 280ff.

64. Whitehead contends that the body is continuous with the rest of the natural world, and the brain is continuous with the body (AI 225). Thus the occasion of experience is within the world and the world is within the occasion, even though the conscious perception of the experience is derived. He explains further:
"Each experient enjoys a perspective apprehension of the world, and equally is an element in the world by reason of this very prehension, which anchors him to a world transcending his own experience. For, it belongs to the nature of this perspective derivation, that the world thus disclosed proclaims its own transcendence of that disclosure [AI 228]."

65. "As entities become . . . less totally dominated by efficient causation and progressively more sensitive to final causation; . . . [t]hey become superjectively oriented; they anticipate the effects of their present decisions on the future and modify their present decisions accordingly; they operate telically in

the light of goals, purposes and ideals. To operate telically in the light of goals, purposes and ideals is to be human. . . ." (Donald W. Sherburne, "Responsibility, Punishment, and Whitehead's Theory of the Self," in Alfred North Whitehead: Essays on His Philosophy, ed. by George L. Kline [Englewood Cliffs: N.J.: Prentice-Hall, 1963], p. 186).

66. A primary way to accomplish this is to initiate a causal route which will contribute to the realization of the desired goal. See Crocker, "A Whiteheadian Theory of Intentions and Actions," pp. 256-63.

67. Douglas Browning, in "Whitehead's Theory of Human Agency," Dialogue, V2, N4 (1964), pp. 424-41, provides an excellent discussion of Whitehead's notion of consciousness in relation to human decision and action, but finds Whitehead inadequate because even though humans are conscious of processes, make decisions, "grow, emerge, concresce, or whatever," they cannot (as Browning reads Whitehead) "act consciously [436-37]." Humans, in Whitehead's perspective, are "only the determinant of processes, and [for Browning] this is not enough [437]." For Browning, the human agent must somehow be able to "act" in a way which is transcendent of, or at least not a "sub-process of concrescence [437]." On the other hand, that intentional actions are possible in a Whiteheadian scheme is systematically developed by Crocker, in "A Whiteheadian Theory of Intentions and Actions."

68. Svensson, in "The Concept of Change," pp. 280ff, calls this "anticipatory activity."

69. In this context, Baldwin, in "Evil and Persuasive Power," p. 271, notes that "pollution, population, and the energy crisis are examples of situations demanding responsible free choice expecting consequences remote in time."

70. See also Sherburne, "Responsibility, Punishment, and Whitehead's Theory of the Self," pp. 179-89, and Daniel D. Williams, "Moral Obligation in Process Philosophy," in Alfred North Whitehead: Essays on His Philosophy, ed. by George L. Kline (Englewood Cliffs, N.J.: Prentice-Hall, 1963), pp. 190-95.

71. ". . . the final decision of the immediate subject-superject, constituting the ultimate modification of subjective aim, is the foundation of our experience of responsibility, of approbation or of disapprobation, of self approval or of self-reproach, of freedom, of emphasis [PR 74]."

72. See especially Adventures of Ideas, pp. 241-96.

73. For example, see DuBois, "Reason in Ethics: A Whiteheadian Perspective," in Johnson, Whitehead's Theory of Reality, pp. 97-118.

74. We have discussed the social nature of reality at length earlier in the chapter.

75. For further discussion see Johnson, Whitehead's Philosophy in Civilization, pp. 11, 12 & 97; and Victor Lowe, "The Concept of Experience in Whitehead's Metaphysics," in Alfred North Whitehead: Essays on His Philosophy, ed. by George L. Kline (Englewood Cliffs, N.J.: Prentice-Hall, 1963), pp. 124ff.

76. "The individual immediacy of an occasion is the final unity of subjective form, which is the occasion as an absolute reality. This immediacy is its moment of sheer individuality, bounded on either side by essential relativity. The occasion arises from relevant objects, and perishes into the status of an object for other occasions. But it enjoys its decisive moment of absolute self-attainment as emotional unity [AI 177]."

77. The five qualities of intense and harmonious experience are Truth, Beauty, Adventure, Art, and Peace (AI 285). For Whitehead's explanation of these qualities see Adventures of Ideas, pp. 241-96.

78. "The watchwords of the nineteenth century have been, struggle for existence, competition, class warfare, commercial antago-nism between nations, military warfare. The struggle for existence has been construed into the gospel of hate. The full conclusion to be drawn from a philosophy of evolution is fortunately of a more balanced character. Successful organisms modify their environment. Those organisms are successful which modify their environment, so as to assist each other [SMW 205]."

79. We have discussed the emergence of consciousness, and the capacity to reason via negative judgments, and to reason inductively and reflectively in the context of praxis. We have noted the social nature of reality and the locus of value. In this context we can understand Whitehead when he writes:

"I now state the thesis that the explanation of this active attack on the environment is a three-fold urge: (i) to live, (ii) to live well, (iii) to live better. In fact the art of life is first to be alive, secondly to be alive in a satisfactory way, and thirdly to acquire an increase in satisfaction. It is at this point of our argument that we have to recur to the function of Reason, namely the promotion of the art of life. The primary function of Reason is the direction of the attack on the environment [FR 8]."

80. ". . . civilization in its aim at fineness of feeling should so arrange its social relations, and the relations of its members

to their natural environment, as to evoke into the experiences of its members Appearances dominated by the harmonies of forceful enduring things [AI 282]."

81. For further discussion see Baldwin, "Evil and Persuasive Power," p. 268.

82. Svensson, in "The Concept of Change," p. 207, writes: "If the planner is to intervene consciously in the social matrix, the attribution of meaning must be articulated as knowledge." Svensson is simply saying that if we are going to "plan" meaningful experience, we must have "knowledge" as to what conjunctions of physical and conceptual actuality produce, or are productive of "meaningful" experience.

83. I mean here that free health care would have to be institutionalized in order to structure, or "form and control," the delivery of that care. For a discussion of institutions and structures from a Whiteheadian perspective, see Sullivan, "The Process Social Paradigm and the Problem of Social Order," pp. 80ff.

84. "It is a false dichotomy to think of nature and Man. Mankind is that factor in Nature which exhibits in its most intense form the plasticity of nature. Plasticity is the introduction of novel law [AI 78]."
Sullivan, in "The Process Social Paradigm and the Problem of Social Order," writes: ". . . the whole of Whitehead's social philosophy is based on the doctrine of Immanent Law, which sees society as founded on interaction [21]." He goes on to write that Whitehead's theory "consistently places social discussions against the background of the continuum of nature [21], and that it provides the elements for a theory "of the human individual as a social reality [25]."

85. For an interesting discussion of a "philosophy of nature," as it pertains more explicitly to the philosophy of science, see Ivor Leclerc, "The Necessity Today of the Philosophy of Nature," Process Studies, V3, N3 (Fall, 1973), pp. 158-168.

86. Johnson's book, Whitehead's Philosophy of Civilization, is a description of Whitehead's images of "civilization." This is to be distinguished from a social theory drawn from Whitehead's philosophy of organism. Whitehead's contribution, like Marx's contribution, is to understanding the social, historical process; and it is as risky to focus on Whitehead's images of the end product, as it is to focus on Marx's, since that is missing the point made so well by Whitehead himself: "The proper test is not that of finality, but of progress [PR 21]." This is not to say, (i) that the nature of the process, e.g., the social nature of reality and the subjective nature of experience, is not, by nature, demanding of a certain type of

civilization, (ii) that Whitehead didn't see that, nor (iii) that his projections as to what civilization should look like are not helpful; it is to say, however, that his images of "civilization" are more reflective of a liberal gentleman than they are of a rigorous application of his philosophy of organism to social theory. Furthermore, Johnson and others concerned with a Whiteheadian perspective of civilization or culture (e.g., Hall, "The Civilization of Experience: A Whiteheadian Theory of Culture"), usually draw most heavily from Adventures of Ideas, which by design is concerned with the "intellectual agencies" or general ideas and specialized notions involved in the modification of historical epochs (AI 12). It is thus concerned with the history of culture (AI 8), and more aptly is a counter-point to Marx's Grundrisse, than a balanced philosophy of civilization.

THE PLACE OF THE HUMAN CAPACITY TO INTERVENE
IN THE PROCESS OF HUMAN HISTORY AS DEVELOPED
IN MARXIST THEORY

In Chapter I I reviewed some of the major categories of Whitehead's philosophy in the context of the question of human conscious intervention in the historical process, with the aim of translating and applying Whitehead's philosophy to this aspect of social theory. This chapter is a discussion of Marxist theory in the context of the same question. I will discuss relevant Marxist categories, assumptions, methods, and conclusions; and I will make note of divergent Marxist positions and of parallels between Marxist theory and Whitehead's philosophy. I will postpone to Chapter III both the discussion of the relevant areas of divergence between process theory and Marxist theory, and the identification and explication of the problem areas in Marxist theory which this study will address. I will then discuss the divergencies in the context of six problem areas or unresolved questions in Marxist theory which are relevant to the problem of this study.

In Chapters II and III I will attempt to be comprehensive, with reference to the questions of this study, in the research of Marx's writings and in representing the range of positions in Marxist theory.[1]

A. Consciousness in Marxist Theory

1. Consciousness in Relation to the Givenness of History, i.e., Historical Materialism

In January 1859, after years of research and eight years before the first volume of Das Kapital, Karl Marx summarizes the "conclusion" and "guiding principle" of his studies:

> The general conclusion at which I arrived and which, once reached, became the guiding principle of my studies can be summarized as follows. In the social production of their existence, men inevitably enter into definite relations, which are independent of their will, namely relations of production appropriate to

a given stage in the development of their material forces of production. The totality of these relations of production constitutes the economic structure of society, the real foundation, on which arises a legal and political superstructure and to which correspond definite forms of social consciousness. The mode of production of material life conditions the general process of social, political and intellectual life. It is not the consciousness of men that determines their existence, but their social existence that determines their consciousness.[2]

This is the appropriate place for this study to begin the discussion of Marx. However it must be noted that this is the summary of a guiding principle, not the total of his philosophy. Furthermore this quotation should not be understood as a statement reflecting a mechanistic materialism[3] or a definitive statement on the role of ideology, human creativity or consciousness. As we will see, Marx's materialism--like Whitehead's of three-quarters of a century later--is organic and based on experience, and the experience of humanity in the evolution of Nature.

Historical materialism, or the dialectical materialist interpretation of history, is the guiding principle of Marxist social and economic theory. Marx understands humans and nature as internally and externally related,[4] and humanity's development as a unique historical aspect of natural history. To understand materialism as Marx understood it, it is necessary to discard conventional notions of materialism. As Marx develops the concept it does not mean the reduction of all human activity to crude matter,[5] nor does it refer to the passive, or selfish baser motives of persons. Parallel to our discussion of Whitehead, Marx means that life and conscious thinking have their origin in non-thinking matter, and that under certain conditions organic life comes forth out of inorganic matter.

In this context, then, human labor is the focal point; what is produced, how it is produced and how persons are related to themselves, others, and the rest of nature determine the basis and limits of their existence. It follows, for Marx, that production and relations of production are the basis of our social and political institutions, our ideas and to a significant degree the natural world around us. As new forces of production and relations of production emerge, so too do institutional forms,

ideologies, and politics which will be more compatible
with the new forces of production. It is in this movement
or process of history that conscious humans find themselves; and it is within this process and amidst these
forces that humans must act if they wish to intervene
consciously in their historical process.

In his discussion on Feuerbach in The German Ideology, Marx sets down the "four moments" or "four aspects of
the primary historical relationships," which we have
discussed above, and in which conscious persons find
themselves.[6] Marx states the first premise thus:

> . . . the first premise of all human existence
> and, therefore, of all history, the premise,
> namely, that men must be in a position to live
> in order to be able to "make history". But life
> involves before everything else eating and
> drinking, a habitation, clothing and many other
> things. The first historical act is thus the
> production of the means to satisfy these needs,
> the production of material life itself [GI 48].

"History," for Marx, is human history, and it begins when
humans begin to distinguish themselves from the animal
world. This position is clear in his second point below;
it must be noted however that human history, while unique
amidst nature, is not above, or separate from nature.

> The second point is that the satisfaction of
> the first need (the action of satisfying, and
> the instrument of satisfaction which has been
> acquired) leads to new needs; . . .
> The third circumstance which, from the very
> outset, enters into historical development, is
> that men, who daily remake their own life,
> begin to make other men, to propagate their
> kind: the relation between man and woman,
> parents and children, the family. The family,
> which to begin with is the only social rela-
> tionship, becomes later, when increased needs
> create a new social relations and the increased
> population new needs, a subordinate one. . .
> and must then be treated and analyzed according
> to the existing empirical data, not according
> to 'the concept of the family,' . . . [GI 49].

That is to say, as human history develops and the production of products and needs increases, persons organize
themselves, not only for propagation of the species but

for production, distribution and socio-political structuring of that production and distribution. Marx's concern is that social structures such as the family be analyzed and understood as a "relation" within the productive-reproductive process, and not as the manifestation of a "concept," i.e., the concept must be understood as a manifestation and description of an emergent historic structure of relations, and not vice versa. This should not be understood to say that once a concept has emerged it is not a real force in history[7] nor as we will see, that concepts which originate in human consciousness cannot be actualized through human activity. This will be discussed at length below.

We begin to see (i) the abstract philosophical foundation and meaning in Marx's social analysis, and (ii) the similarity between his world-view and Whitehead's philosophical scheme when Marx writes:

> These three aspects of social activity are not of course to be taken as three different stages, but just as three aspects or, to make it clear to the Germans, three "moments", which have existed simultaneously since the dawn of history and the first men, and which still assert themselves in history today [GI 50].

Here and more extensively in The Grundrisse, we find Marx discussing abstractions of, or "moments" in, a "process." This language is very anticipatory of Whitehead's "phases" in the development of an actual entity. The "moments" and "phases" in each instance refer to abstract elements of a process, which presuppose and require each other and the whole; and which assist us in understanding the process of the integrated whole.

The fourth moment is the emergence of society in the context of the influence of the integrated natural and social environment. Marx writes:

> The production of life, both of one's own in labour and of fresh life in procreation, now appears as a double relationship: on the one hand as a natural, on the other as a social relationship. By social we understand the cooperation of several individuals, no matter under what conditions, in what manner and to what end. It follows from this that a certain mode of production, or industrial stage, is always combined with a certain mode of coopera-

tion, or social stage, and this mode of cooperation is itself a "productive force". Further, that the multitude of productive forces accessible to men determines the nature of society, hence, that the "history of humanity" must always be studied and treated in relation to the history of industry and exchange [GI 50].

It is only and always in the context of the material (natural and social) world that Marx discusses the emergence of consciousness;[8] which like language "only arises from the need, the necessity, of intercourse with other men [GI 51]." "Consciousness is therefore, from the very beginning a social product, and remains so as long as men exist at all [GI 51]."

I have introduced Marx's understanding of the givenness of history as historical materialism, and I have noted its various aspects which provide a foundation for the emergence of consciousness. Marx's understanding of the givenness of history, however, deserves (with reference to the problem of this study) further discussion from the perspectives of (i) the social nature of reality, (ii) the species-nature of humans, and (iii) the nature of history as process.

The social nature of reality.[9] The social nature of reality, in Marx's writings, can be discussed from various perspectives; these include (a) the organic relation of humans to nature, (b) the social nature which describes the relation of individuals to other individuals and the community (this is very close to "species-being" which will be discussed in more detail below), (c) the social relationship between individuals in productive society, and (d) the social relationship of individuals as objectified in money, and as objectified and dominated by developed relational structures and instruments of production; this last category has a close parallel in Whitehead's category of efficient causation, as applied to social theory.[10]

Marx's clearest expression of humanity's organic and social relationship to nature is set forth in the Economic and Philosophical Manuscripts, where he writes:

> The universality of man appears in practice in the universality which makes the whole of nature into his inorganic body: (1) as a direct means of life; and equally (2) as the material object and instrument of his life activity.

> Nature is the inorganic body of man; that is to
> say nature, excluding the human body itself.
> To say that man _lives_ from nature means that
> nature is his _body_ with which he must remain in
> a continuous interchange in order not to die.
> The statement that the physical and mental life
> of man, and nature, are interdependent means
> simply that nature is interdependent with it-
> self, for man is a part of nature [EPM 126-27].

This quotation is important for our discussion because it
is representative of Marx's understanding and his reasoning with reference to the oneness of the world, and it
demonstrates the holistic unity of humanity and nature
from which consciousness will emerge.[11]

Marx's understanding of materialism places humanity
within, and as part and product of, nature.[12] But humans
have created societies and a history, with productive
forces and social structures. Thus humans are social in
nature also by virtue of the fact that they are products
of their social environment, just as they are of their
ecological environment. Marx writes:

> We have seen how . . . man produces man,
> himself and then other men; how the object
> which is the direct activity of his personality
> is at the same time his existence for other men
> and their existence for him. Similarly, the
> material of labour and man himself as a subject
> are the starting-point as well as the result of
> this movement (and because there must be this
> starting-point private property is a histori-
> cal necessity). Therefore, the _social_ charac-
> ter is the universal character of the whole
> movement; _as_ society itself produces _man_ as
> _man_, so it _is produced_ by him. Activity and
> mind are social in their content as well as in
> their _origin_; they are _social_ activity and
> social _mind_. The _human_ significance of nature
> only exists for _social_ man, because only in
> this case is nature a _bond_ with other _men_, the
> basis of his existence for others and _of_ their
> existence for him. Only then is nature the
> _basis_ of his own _human_ experience and a vital
> element of human _reality_. The _natural_ exist-
> ence of man has here become his _human_ existence
> and nature itself has become human for him.
> Thus _society_ is the accomplished union of man
> with nature, the veritable resurrection of

nature, the realized naturalism of man and the realized humanism of nature [EPM 157].

The above quotation is drawn from a discussion of the nature of humans in the context of a productive community; a productive community presently structured as capitalistic, with the existence of "private property." Habermas argues that Marx's "image of man" was not a concern with the "objective essence" and the "essential" capacities of a "being of nature"; the character of which "can be interpreted anthropologically or even in terms of fundamental ontology, as a constant structure." He argues that Marx's image of man "was developed as a specific analysis of a concrete situation, namely that of the 'condition of the working class'" under capitalism as he knew it.[13] The point here is that Marx's theory does have an image or nature of man; it is however historical not "ontological" in a metaphysical sense.

In the context of capitalism, Marx says that material and mental activity are social in their content as well as their origin. Humans have developed their productive society, and, as I noted above, that society, in a social sense, is not simply nature and human individuals, but also includes created relational structures, e.g., the division of labor, and the exchanging of produce via the institution of money. Money in this sense is both a created institution of social relations and an objective form, which now exists and participates in the social environment of humans with the force of what Whitehead called efficient causation. Marx, in The Grundrisse, proivdes an extensive discussion of how created economic relations of exchange gain "independence," (or objectivity) and in turn determine how humans relate, act and think, with each other. He writes:

> The reciprocal and all-sided dependence of individuals who are indifferent to one another forms their social connection. This social bond is expressed in exchange value, by means of which alone each individual's own activity or his product becomes an activity and a product for him; he must produce a general product--exchange value, or, the latter isolated for itself and individualized, money. On the other side, the power which each individual exercises over the activity of others or over social wealth exists in him as the owner of exchange values, of money. The individual carries his social power, as well as his bond with society, in his pocket. . . .

> The social character of activity, as well as the social form of the product, and the share of individuals in production here appear as something alien and objective, confronting the individuals, not as their relation to one another, but as their subordination to relations which subsist independently of them and which arise out of collisions between mutually indifferent individuals.[14]

Money thus becomes the "objectified relation between persons" (Grundrisse 160).[15] And as such it enters as a determining form in the social process. This reference to money is important for our discussion at two points: (i) the structuring of mutual relations of people's productive activities is a primary factor to be considered by any person attempting to intervene in the historical process, and (ii) it is an excellent example of a social form which gains objectivity and thus efficiently causal status, with the resulting effect upon actuality and consciousness of individuals. The objectified social relation, i.e., the money relation, which has gained some independent determining influence over individuals is, of course, an abstraction. The abstraction, or idea (i.e., money), is however nothing more than the "theoretical expression" of real material relations, which must be materially as well as conceptually changed if persons' real life experiences are to be changed.

As persons, in their social nature, are related to nature, to other humans, and to their objectified material relations, so they are to the things which they create.[16] And as humans may become ruled by their structures of relationship, so they can become subjects of the material objects which they create. "To exclude either side of this internal relation between man and his products (such that each may be seen to dominate the other) is to arrive at a dead end, in one instance of 'vulgar determinism' and in the other of equally vulgar 'free will'."[17] As Whitehead noted that once the steam engine had been created, it became a determinant force for the future of the west, so in parallel fashion, Marx in Capital notes how "furnaces and workshops," in the capitalist mode of production, affect human activity, relations and consciousness. He writes:

> It is now no longer the labourer that employs the means of production, but the means of production that employ the labourer. . . . Furnaces and workshops that stand idle by night,

and absorb no living labour, are "a mere loss" to the capitalist. Hence, furnaces and work-shops constitute lawful claims upon the night-labour of the workpeople. . . . [T]his complete inversion of the relation between dead and living labour, between value and the force that creates value, mirrors itself in the con-sciousness of the capitalists.[18]

As Marx writes later in Capital: "the instrument of labour becomes the means of enslaving, exploiting, and impover-ishing the labourer [Capital I 506]." In both of these passages Marx is criticizing capitalism; he speaks of the relation between human products and humans in a given political-economic system, but even when and if the structures are reversed and the instruments of labor become the means of human development, Marx would still speak of the definitive relation between the products and the people.

Finally it must be noted that the givenness of history out of which consciousness emerges also includes ideas and concepts. We will discuss the origin and function of ideas more below, but as it was important when reviewing Whitehead to note that concepts and ideas are emergent in history and that once created they can be a historical force, thus it is important to note the place of ideas, in the givenness of history, in Marxist theo-ry.[19]

Marx in his critique of Proudhon, notes that people create their "ideas, categories" just as they do their social relations and linen and silks; and that the ideas are "historical and transitory" just as are other crea-tions.[20] But his most powerful statements on "ideas" come from the German Ideology, where he writes, for example:

The production of ideas, of conceptions, of consciousness, is at first directly interwoven with the material activity and the material intercourse of men, the language of real life. Conceiving, thinking, the mental intercourse of men, appear at this stage as the direct efflux of their material behaviour. The same applies to mental production as expressed in the language of politics, laws, morality, re-ligion, metaphysics, etc.--real, active men, as they are conditioned by a definite develop-ment of their productive forces and of the intercourse corresponding to these, up to its furthest forms. Consciousness can never be anything else than conscious existence, and the existence of men is their actual life-process [GI 47].

Once conceptions, which have their source in individuals and work conditions (GI 65), are created, they can become material forces, exercising their influence on the process of history in several ways. Ideas may function conservatively as the "ruling ideas" of the ruling class (GI 64-65), or the "tradition of all the dead generations."[21] Created ideas, as theory, can also function as a "radical" "material force" for revolutionary masses,[22] or simply as the "ideas" which describe, project and finally give directive form to "practical force."[23]

Ideas are also the conceptual form (for consciousness) of sense experience by which humans such as Marx and Whitehead are able to do natural and human science (EPM 163-64), and by which people make propositional judgments.[24] The functions of ideas, concepts and theories will be discussed (in relation to consciousness) in more detail below; the important point here is to establish that in Marx's theory--as in Whitehead's, if not to the same degree--ideas or theories are influential historical parts, or functional abstract aspects, of the givenness of historical human reality, as are things, social relations, persons and nature.[25] These abstract (and real) aspects form the determinant source or origin (social environment) of physical, conscious human persons, and must be considered as determinant variables to be accounted for, by any person who wishes to intervene consciously in the process of history.

Species-being. The category which Marx uses to discuss the special natural-social relationship which humans have with each other, as over against their relation to their environment in general, is "species-being."[26] This category deserves special attention because it is the real philosophical foundation for humanistic socialism in Marx's work.

For Marx, if humans are to fulfill their "true," "authentic" "human nature," they must do so in social and productive cooperation as citizens with other citizens in community.[27] It is particularly in the sphere of productive relations that individuals actualize their species-being; this is why Marx is so critical of the "Rights of Man." He writes:

> . . . the Rights of Man do not, . . . free man
> from religion but give him the freedom of re-
> ligion; . . . they do not free him from proper-
> ty, but procure for him freedom of property;
> . . . they do not free him from the filth of gain
> but give him freedom of choice of a livelihood
> [HF 152].28

Thus the Rights of Man do not acknowledge the species-being of persons, but rather posit society and other persons as "external," and elevate "private interest," preservation of property and egoistic feeling above communal interests (JQ 26). The right of property becomes the right of existence. When this individual liberty forms the basis of civil society, "[i]t leads every man to see in other men, not the realization, but rather the limitations of his own liberty [JQ 25]." Liberty and fulfillment thus become founded not on "the relations between man and man, but rather upon the separation of man from man [JQ 24-25]."

The concept of the species-character of persons is manifested in production and self-production by the fact that an individual through one's labor can be objectified in a commodity which is a need for another individual and vice versa. Thus he writes that these persons stand "in a social relation to one another [Grundrisse 243]." He continues:

> This is not all. The fact that this need on the
> part of one can be satisfied by the product of
> the other, and vice versa, and that the one is
> capable of producing the object of the need of
> the other, and that each confronts the other as
> owner of the object of the other's need, this
> proves that each of them reaches beyond his own
> particular need etc., as a human being, and
> that they relate to one another as human
> beings; that their common species-being [Gat-
> tungswesen] is acknowledged by all [Grundrisse
> 243].29

This is not, for Marx, the same as when "elephants produce for tigers, or animals for other animals [Grundrisse 243]," partially because the individuals are equals, but also because they recognize one another "reciprocally as proprietors" and thus exchange needs via freedom and not by force.

Even more importantly, in this process, individuals come to realize themselves as both ends-in-themselves and means for others as ends-in-themselves, and that individual self interests if properly understood coincide with common or general interest.[30] Marx writes:

> Each serves the other in order to serve himself; each makes use of the other, reciprocally, as his means. Now both things are contained in the consciousness of the two individuals: (i) that each arrives at his end only in so far as he serves the other as means; (2) that each becomes means for the other (being for another) . . . only as end in himself (being for self) . . . (3) that the reciprocity in which each is at the same time means and end, and attains his end only in so far as he becomes a means, and becomes a means only in so far as he posits himself as end, that each thus posits himself as being for another, in so far as he is being for self, and the other as being for him, in so far as he is being for himself--that this reciprocity is a necessary fact, presupposed as natural precondition of exchange, but that, as such, it is irrelevant to each of the two subjects in exchange, and that this reciprocity interests him only in so far as it satisfied his interest to the exclusion of, without reference to, that of the other. That is, the common interest which appears as the motive of the act as a whole is recognized as a fact by both sides; but, as such, it is not the motive, but rather proceeds, as it were, behind the back of one individual's interest in opposition to that of the other. In this last respect, the individual can at most have the consoling awareness that the satisfaction of his antithetical individual interest is precisely the realization of the suspended antithesis, of the social, general interest [Grundrisse 243-44].

In Marx's understanding, humans cannot change the fact that their nature and their productive existence is now social and species in character; that is not to say that they cannot frustrate the full development of that nature and alienate themselves from each other, themselves and their products, or that it makes no difference whether or not they are conscious of the species-character of their beings. The first of these two points is amply demonstrated in history, and the second will be discussed at length later in this chapter. What is important to establish here is that throughout Marx's writings, discussions of alienation are discussions of the frustration of the development of the species-life of individuals[31] and that human fulfillment always requires the development of species-life.[32] From a Marxist perspective, then, persons who wish to have conscious perceptions which accurately reflect the nature of reality, and who wish to intervene consciously and effectively in the process of history will think and act with the species-character of humans as one of the givens of history. To do otherwise would be to alienate human relationships and stifle the actualization of human needs and capacities as they have developed in human nature.

The nature of history as process.[33] In discussing the nature of reality and the nature of the process or movement of history, the most pronounced parallel between Marx and Whitehead comes in a comparison of the Grundrisse and Process and Reality. The point here is that Marx, in the Grundrisse, in discussing capital, production, circulation and money, uses an organic-process model which is very similar to Whitehead's cosmological model. Marx uses the model through this long preparatory work to Capital. Referring to the whole of a society over a long period of time, Marx writes:

> When we consider bourgeois society in the long view and as a whole, then the final result of the process of social production always appears as the society itself, i.e., the human being itself in its social relations. Everything that has a fixed form, such as the product etc., appears as merely a moment, a vanishing moment, in this movement. The direct production process itself here appears only as a moment. The conditions and objectifications of the process are themselves equally moments of it, and its only subjects are the individuals, but individuals in mutual relationships, which they equally reproduce and produce anew. The constant process of their own movement, in which they renew themselves even as they renew the world of wealth they create [Grundrisse 712].

Notice in this quotation the reference to things that have fixed "forms" and the appearance of vanishing "moments." The use of "form" here is nearly identical to Whitehead's use of the category; particularly when it is applied to a moment, i.e., in this sense a particular form of actual

73

occasion which has persistent reoccurence. What is persistent is the form, not the particular occasion. "Product" is such a form or "eternal object".[34]

Now let us look at a smaller (than society) scale application, viz., the production process.

> The total production process of capital includes both the circulation process proper and the actual production process. These form the two great sections of its movement, which appears as the totality of these two processes. On one side, labour time, on the other, circulation time. And the whole of the movement appears as unity of labour time and circulation time, as unity of production and circulation. This unity itself is motion, process. Capital appears as this unity-in-process of production and circulation, as unity which can be regarded both as the totality of the process of its production, as well as the specific completion of one turnover of the capital, one movement returning into itself [Grundrisse 620].

"Actual production" here finds its parallel in the internal development and concrescence of an actual entity, in Whitehead. As the emergence of an actual occasion is both a process for itself and the future, and an entity (moment or datum) for others, and as both a process for itself and the future, and an entity (moment or datum) for others, so in like fashion Marx speaks of production (and its conditions and objectifications) as both a process and a moment in the social process, with the subject in this instance being the persons who are themselves involved in the productive and reproductive process of actualizing themselves for themselves and for the world around them. "Circulation" finds its parallel in the status of actual entities which have become objective data for others in their relevant future. Labor time is analogous to the time, energy and activity of the emerging actual entity in the stage when it is creative of itself. The circulation time is analogous to that time following concrescence when the objective entity is data for new occasions. Marx simply and accurately describes the total productive process of capital as a unity-in-process in which the various forms of capital continue to go through continual production-circulation-production-circulation.

He reduces the scale of the model further, and discusses the production process in terms of the moments of material, labor, and product; or in Whiteheadian terms, the datum, subject and superject. He writes:

> . . . the raw material is consumed by being changed, formed by labour, and the instrument of labour is consumed by being used up in this process, worn out. On the other hand, labour also is consumed by being employed, set into motion, and a certain amount of the worker's muscular force etc. is thus expended, so that he exhausts himself. But labour is not only consumed, but also at the same time fixed, converted from the form of activity into the form of the object; materialized; as a modification of the object, it modifies its own form and changes from activity to being. The end of the process is the product, in which the raw material appears as bound up with labour, and in which the instrument of labour has, likewise, transposed itself from a mere possibility into a reality, by having become a real conductor of labour, but thereby also having been consumed in its static form through its mechanical or chemical relation to the material of labour. All three moments of the process, the material, the instrument, and labour, coincide in the neutral result - the product. The moments of the process of production which have been consumed to form the product are simultaneously reproduced in it. The whole process therefore appears as productive consumption, i.e. as consumption which terminates neither in a void, nor in the mere subjectification of the objective, but which is, rather, again posited as an object. . . . This form-giving activity consumes the object and consumes itself, but it consumes the given form of the object only in order to posit it in a new objective form, and it consumes itself only in its subjective form as activity. It consumes the objective character of the object - the indifference towards the form - and the subjective character of activity; forms the one, materializes the other. . . . [Grundrisse 300-01].

Raw materials, which include previously created products, are merged with instruments of labor, i.e., tools and machines which are also previously created products, through the activity and energy of living subjective labor, to create a new product. The product will be consumed as material for a new product, instruments of labor, or by the laborer to create new labor power. In this way the various moments "determine each other internally" (Grundrisse 414), even though each moment, in some sense and during some time, has its own objective identity, and thus externality, with reference to the other factors in the process.[35]

Thus we find in Marxist theory a worldview which is holistic, social, emergent and self-creative. Nature, humanity, created tools, structures of relations, and ideas all gain objectivity and thus have in some sense external relations to each other; and yet they are all related internally because at some point in the process they are parts of a whole, as well as, the source and the product of the ongoing process. Furthermore their form at any moment has its meaning only within the whole.[36]

History is not personified, and it does not act. People are unique by virtue of their species-character, and their unique capacity to create consciously their environment and themselves,[37] albeit within the givenness of history. Marx writes:

> Men make their own history, but they do not make it just as they please; they do not make it under circumstances chosen by themselves, but under circumstances directly encountered, given and transmitted from the past. The tradition [physical, structural and mental] of all the dead generations weighs like a nightmare on the brain of the living [18th Brumaire 15].

Nonetheless the brain of the living human has the capacity of consciousness, and the power to direct history-making activity. In this context, Habermas convincingly argues that for Marx: "The meaning of history as a whole is revealed theoretically to the degree to which mankind practically undertakes to make with will and consciousness that history which it has always made anyhow."[38]

I have discussed the Marxist view of the given world in which consciousness emerges; let me now turn to a discussion which focuses on the place and function of ideas and concepts in Marxist writings, in light of the problem of this study.

76

2. Consciousness in Relation to Ideas, Concepts, Categories and Values

I noted earlier in this chapter that ideas are created by humans as they create their social relations and products, and as they shape their environment. I also noted that ideas can function conservatively or radically, and also as the conceptual tools for doing science and making value judgments. In this section I will discuss ideas as categories or forms, and elaborate on the above points as I try to understand the relationship of a conscious person to his/her and society's ideas.

Marx begins with the assumption of a real, actual world which brings forth humans who create human history and in that process create ideas; not out of nothing, but out of, and in conjunction with, their emergent selves and nature. Lenin draws on Engels to make this point. He writes: "Anybody who reads Anti-Duhring and Ludwig Feuerbach with the slightest care will find scores of instances when Engels speaks of things and their reflections [image, idea or form] in the human brain, in our consciousness, thought, etc."[39]

Many of Marx's statements concerning ideas, and mind were, as is well known, in reaction to the notion that ideas and/or mind had independent and perhaps even autonomous existence apart from the actual, natural world. Marx's well known position on this issue is represented by this quotation from the early pages of Capital:

> My dialectic method is not only different from the Hegelian, but is its direct opposite. To Hegel, the life-process of the human brain, i.e., the process of thinking, which, under the name of 'the Idea,' he even transforms into an independent subject, is the demi-urgos of the real world, and the real world is only the external, phenomenal form of 'the Idea.' With me, on the contrary, the ideal is nothing else than the material world reflected by the human mind, and translated into forms of thought [Capital I 19].[40]

Engels, in Anti-Duhring, spells out his understanding of the merits and the limits of Hegel's contribution. Its merit was that for the first time

> The whole natural, historical and spiritual world was presented as a process, that is, as

in constant motion, change, transformation and development; and the attempt was made to show the internal interconnections in this motion and development.[41]

Hegel, however, had a severe limitation, i.e., he was an idealist, and the result was that his "system as such was a colossal miscarriage."[42]

The problem of being an idealist was that

the thoughts within his mind were to him not the more or less abstract images of real things and processes, but, on the contrary, things and their development were to him only the images made real of the "idea" existing somewhere or other already before the world existed.[43]

For Marx, the idea is the material world reflected by the human mind and translated into forms of thought. Ideas are internal, mental forms which reflect the forms of the real world. Lenin states this position (in his reaction against idealism), with its implications for theory of knowledge:

Our sensation, our consciousness is only an image of the external world, and it is obvious that an image cannot exist without the thing imaged, and that the latter exists independently of that which images it. Materialism deliberately makes the "naive" belief of mankind the foundation of its theory of knowledge.[44]

Mao also maintains this understanding of materialism and the origin of, and grounding of, consciousness. He writes:

If we consider this thing known as consciousness in the light of thoroughgoing materialism (that is to say in the light of materialist dialectics), then what we call consciousness is nothing else but a form of the movement of matter, a particular characteristic of the material brain of humanity; it is that particular characteristic of the material brain which causes the material processes outside consciousness to be reflected in consciousness.[45]

The first point here is that the world is real. The second is that the forms or structures and shapes of the real world are historical and transitory as is the world.[46] The third point is that ideas, categories and mental forms are either accurate conceptions or mental forms, which accurately reflect the world, or inaccurate conceptualizations of the perceptions of the real world. I will discuss the problem of verification later in this chapter, in our discussion of praxis.

The ideas or categories thus are the "abstract ideal expressions" of the way the real world is in actuality. And since I have already shown that Marx holds the productive sphere of social life to be its foundation, it is not surprising that the ideas, forms or categories with which his major work is concerned are contemporary (for him), productive and economic categories or forms, e.g., property, commodity, money, and capital.[47] If we can understand how Marx, in a philosophical tradition from Plato through Hegel, used and modified the understanding of ideas and forms, we will be closer to understanding how persons (within the Marxist scheme) can intervene consciously in the historical process.

First, it is important to note that Marx is clear that each idea, and therefore any discussion of categories, or of society, is only an abstract perspective of a real whole. He writes:

> In the succession of the economic categories, as in any other historical, social science, it must not be forgotten that their subject -- here, modern bourgeois society--is always what is given, in the head as well as in reality, and that these categories, therefore express the forms of being, the characteristics of existence, and often only individual sides of this specific society, this subject, and that therefore this society by no means begins only at the point where one can speak of it as such; . . . [Grundrisse 106].

The categories thus are abstract and limited mental expressions of actual forms of being, by which we live and can understand our lives. Now let me examine what Marx does with some of these categories.

Property. Property like language is a social relationship and the product of individuals in community (Grundrisse 490). And as a category, "property" is the form of thought used to express a relationship which exists between and among individuals, and between individuals and conditions and materials of production. Marx writes thus of the origin and nature of property:

> Property thus originally means no more than a human being's relation to his natural conditions of production as belonging to him, as his, as presupposed along with his own being; relations to them as natural presuppositions of his self, which only form, so to speak, his extended body. He actually does not relate to his conditions of production, but rather has a double existence, both subjectively as he himself, and objectively in these natural nonorganic conditions of his existence. The forms of these natural conditions of production are double: (1) his existence as a member of a community; . . . (2) the relation to land and soil mediated by the community, . . . [Grundrisse 491-92].

"Property" thus as an idea, principle or category has its origin in the actual relation of the working individual to the conditions of his/her production and reproduction, in the context of community. The forms of property will vary according to the conditions and other relations of production (Grundrisse 495), and the form of the idea will change accordingly. The point of this reference to property is to illustrate in Marx the origin and grounding of categories in the material world, and the relational character of the forms and structures of that world.

Commodity. "Commodity" is the social form which labor takes when people work for one another (Capital I 71). It is also the form which their objectified labor, or the product of their labor takes. In this form,

> . . . the social character of men's labour appears to them as an objective character stamped upon the product of that labour: because the relation of the producers to the sum total of their own labour is presented to them as a social relation, existing not between themselves, but between the products of their labour [Capital I 72].

Thus we see a definite social relation between people that assumes the form of a relation between things. Marx calls this the "Fetishism of commodities"[48] and claims that the analogy is found in the "mist-enveloped regions of the religious world," where "the productions of the human brain appear as independent beings endowed with life, and entering into relation both with one another and the human race [Capital I 72]." So it is, he says, "in the world of commodities with the products of men's hands [Capital I 72]." The result is that human social relations become "material relations between persons [Capital I 73]."

Marx's primary criticism here is of a mode of production in which the products of human labor are given status independent from persons, and in which human labor power is made into a thing, i.e., given a categorical form which is independent of the active person (Grundrisse 310). Later this will be discussed as the problem of reification by Lukacs,[49] and be called the "fallacy of misplaced concreteness" by Whitehead (SMW 51-55). The primary mistake here, according to Marx, is threefold: (i) the only origin of added value is the laboring person,[50] (ii) the locus of value is for Marx always persons and never things, and (iii) specific products and categorical forms are objectified as things in themselves which are not products of human activity and are thus no longer subject to persons, and by implication, cannot be changed and used[51] by humans as they (the persons), develop themselves and create their history. As Marcuse notes, the reification of social relations conceals "their origin, their mechanisms of perpetuation, and the possibility of their transformation. Above all, it conceals their human core and content."[52]

Money. Commodity becomes, in the bourgeois society, the social form of human labor and the products of human labor; and money is the social form of exchange of these commodities. Marx writes:

> . . . the commodity's exchange value obtains a material existence separate from the commodity.
> The definition of a product as exchange value thus necessarily implies that exchange value obtains a separate existence, in isolation from the product. The exchange value which is separated from commodities and exists alongside them as itself a commodity, this is--money. In the form of money, all properties of the commodity as exchange value appear as an object distinct from it, as a form of social existence separated from the natural existence of the commodity [Grundrisse 145].

Money begins as the uniform measure of value for all commodities and as a medium of exchange of these commodities; but it becomes a thing in itself. As Marx notes: "In money the medium of exchange becomes a thing, or, the exchange value of the thing [commodity] achieves an independent existence apart from the thing [Grundrisse 199-200]." And beyond this the original situation is inverted, and real commodities become the representatives of money (Grundrisse 149); or as Marx writes later: "After money is posited as a commodity in reality, the commodity is posited as money in the mind [Grundrisse 191]." But for Marx, "Money is not a thing, it is a social relation [PP 81]." Thus we have another instance of misplaced concreteness, with a historical social relation or form reified as a thing in itself. This reification of categories which reflect social relations is a mental process which reflects an actual although alienated human situation. For Marx, in the first instance, consciousness, e.g., of money as the thing, is an accurate reflection of actual social relations, i.e., money functions as a thing in itself, but it is not a thing in itself, and it is not, in this instance, only because (i) it was and is created by human society, i.e., it is historical and transitory in particular and as a form, and (ii) it can be changed or un-reified by human society in the future. That is to say, alienated society which is structured around "property," "commodity relations" and "money as value" is an actual society, albeit alienating for persons and nature. I will now discuss "capital" in this context and then point out why this discussion of economic and productive categories is important for understanding ideas in Marxist theory.

Capital. "Capital [unlike money] is not a simple relation, but a process in whose various moments it is always capital [Grundrisse 258]." The moments of the process of capital production include (i) material, (ii) labor power, (iii) products, (iv) commodities, and (v) money.[53] Capital is the inclusive category which reflects a type of production; as such it has no actuality independent of its various aspects; but as a mental form which reflects the inclusive process of this type of production it enables persons to conceptualize and reflect on the whole process at once, as well as to see that each of the sub-categories is not a thing in itself, but a moment in a larger social, productive process. Capital as an idea or mental form, and as an actual material and relational process, is (like the sub-categories) real; although man/woman-made, historical and transitory.[54] To say that capital as a process is real is not to say however, that the classical explanation of how that system functions is accurate, e.g., Marx's labor theory of value and its derivative notions give a radically different understanding of the process (Capital I 535ff).

I have discussed here a few of Marx's fundamental economic categories in order to illustrate that Marx's major concern with ideas and categories was not simply to say that they are aspects of a humanly created historical world, but to use ideas and categories (i) to accurately reflect the forces, relations and the nature of human production and reproduction, and (ii) to analyze and expose the social character, historicity and inaccuracy of classical political-economic categories. Thus Marx's analysis uses categories and ideas; and it criticizes both real and conceptual relations and categories. He does not remove ideas or categories from the historical process but defines them as real abstract aspects of a real world. He (i) historicizes both material and conceptual reality, (ii) establishes the radical social nature of physical and conceptual reality, (iii) locates the origin and locus of value in human activity and experience, and (iv) reveals conceptually the real possibility of intentional, conscious human subjugation of the historical process. That is to say, humans already create history and value; what is necessary, for their full social and individual development, is for them to do it intentionally and out of an awareness of their social and species-nature. To do that persons need to understand conceptually the physical and conceptual world in which they live; then they will be able to create, and sustain or change it more effectively for their own benefit. Humans are in Marx's view, "both the authors and the actors of their own drama [HF 115]." The awareness of this point must be the real starting point for understanding, as well as effective intentional action.[55]

Two of the related functions of ideas briefly mentioned earlier now deserve further clarification. First, I will consider the notion that ideas are the conceptual form of experience by which humans are able to do natural and human science. Marx writes:

> One basis for life and another for science is a priori a falsehood. Nature, as it develops in human history, in the act of genesis of human society, is the actual nature of man; thus nature, as it develops through industry, though in an alienated form, is truly anthropological nature.
> ....

Man is the direct object of natural science, because directly <u>perceptible</u> <u>nature</u> is for man directly human sense experience (an identical expression) in the form of the <u>other</u> <u>person</u> who is directly presented to him in a sensuous way. His own sense experience only exists as human sense experience for himself through the <u>other</u> <u>person</u>. But <u>nature</u> is the direct object of the <u>science</u> <u>of</u> <u>man</u>. The first object for man--man himself--is nature, sense experience; and the particular sensuous human faculties, which can only find objective realization in <u>natural</u> objects, can only attain self-knowledge in the science of natural beings. The element of thought itself, the element of the living manifestation of thought, language, is sensuous in character. The <u>social</u> reality of nature and <u>human</u> natural science, or the <u>natural</u> <u>science</u> <u>of</u> <u>man</u>, are identical expressions [EPM 164].

Marx starts from the premise that humanity and nature exist in unity. He adds to this the fact that the natural sciences have developed a "tremendous activity," "assembled an ever-growing mass of data" and have penetrated "<u>practically</u> into human life through industry [EPM 163]." "<u>Industry</u> is [thus] the actual historical relationship of nature, and thus of natural science, to man [EPM 163]." Thus we see that we have a natural science which has proven itself <u>practically</u> through industry which not only links nature and humanity, but by extension provides the basis for a science of humanity. The mode of relationship between humanity and nature by which science functions is perception via the senses. The conceptualization of these sense perceptions[56] provides the "element of thought itself," and the "living manifestation of that thought," i.e., language. This is how Marx reasons it is possible to attain self-knowledge, i.e., ideas, concepts and categories which accurately reflect the "what is" of our material, relational and conceptual world. "What is" is a concept which leads in human perception and thought to the concept of "what is not."[57]

Now we are ready to move to a discussion of how categories facilitate the composition of propositional judgments about reality.[58] Marx's concern is to deal with reality, but he does this with the aid of categories; note his discussion of Proudhon's categories "To Have" and "Not To Have" (HF 59). For Marx, "To Have and Not To Have, wages, salary, want and need, and work to satisfy that need" are categories, but not mere categories. He writes:

> But Not To Have is not a mere category, it is
> a most disconsolate reality; today the man who
> has nothing is nothing, for he is cut off from
> existence in general and still more from a
> human existence; for the condition of having
> nothing is the condition of complete separation
> of man from his objectivity [HF 59].[59]

This real negative judgment of what is not, as linked with
an implicit awareness of human wholeness, is a recurring
theme in Marx's writings, particularly in his analysis of
the exploitation of labor for profit in Capital.[60]

The forces and relations of production, actual socio-political relations and relative ideas and categories
are the subject of Marx's empirical and theoretical
analysis.

In summary we can say, from Marx's own statements and
from his work, that a person who wishes to intervene
consciously in the process of history must (i) understand
the historical and social nature of material and conceptual reality, (ii) analyze and judge the material and
social conditions of human life, (iii) analyze and judge
the accuracy and adequacy of the categories and ideas by
which persons in society understand their economic and
social relations, and (iv) act materially and conceptually to create human material and social conditions; one
significant way to do this is exemplified in Marx's life
work, i.e., to provide for the people an accurate description of their economic and social productive and reproductive process.[61]

3. Consciousness in Relation
to Subjective Freedom

In the beginning of this chapter I quoted the well
known passage from the preface of A Contribution to the
Critique of Political Economy, which reads in part:

> In the social production of their existence,
> men inevitably enter into definite relations,
> which are independent of their will, . . . The
> mode of production of material life conditions
> the general process of social, political and
> intellectual life. It is not the consciousness
> of men that determines their existence, but
> their social existence that determines their
> consciousness [Critique 20-21].

The importance of this quotation is again seen in the 1867 preface of Capital. Marx writes here that he does not want to be understood as being critical of particular personalities but is critical of individuals "only in so far as they are the personifications of economic categories, embodiments of particular class-relations and class-interests [Capital I 10]." He continues:

> My standpoint, from which the evolution of the economic formation of society is viewed as a process of natural history, can less than any other make the individual responsible for relations whose creature he socially remains, however much he may subjectively raise himself above them [Capital I 10].

These two quotations are representative of Marx's perspective of the relation of persons to their natural and social environment. There is in Marx's work (as I noted there is in Whitehead's) a clear understanding that the material, social and conceptual environment in which anyone finds one-self has determinant influence, i.e., a conformal influence on the physical, social and mental makeup and activity of that person. This is, however, for Marx (as for Whitehead), an abstract aspect of the larger theoretical scheme. To say that "social existence determines consciousness" is true but it is not all there is to the truth. To go on to say, as Marx does, that "it is not the consciousness of men that determines their existence" is true in this sense: (i) material existence can be actual without consciousness, (ii) material existence always precedes consciousness, i.e., conscious subjects always find themselves in an already determinate material-social existence and (iii) consciousness, as such, cannot determine existence; consciousness of a person can give direction and motivation to that person's activity which can in turn change his/her material and social existence, that is to say, it is human activity (conscious and unconscious) which is determinant of material and social existence, or human history.[62] This means that if one wishes to change who one is, one must change the material and social existence out of which one lives. This is not mechanistic determinism, but socialistic and dialectical materialism, which understands humans as natural and social but does not remove either will or creativity from persons; rather it puts that will and creativity in a natural, social and historical perspective. Lenin is very clear on this point when he writes:

The idea of determinism, which establishes
the necessity of human acts and rejects the
absurd fable of freedom of will, in no way
destroys man's reason or conscience, or the
judgment of his actions. Quite the contrary,
the determinist view alone makes a strict and
correct judgment possible, instead of attributing everything one fancies to freedom of will.
Similarly, the idea of historical necessity in
no way undermines the role of the individual in
history: all history is made up of the actions
of individuals, who are undoubtedly active
figures. The real question that arises in
judging the social activity of an individual
is: what conditions ensure the success of this
activity, what guarantee is there that this
activity will not remain an isolated act lost
in a welter of contrary acts?[63]

Materialism, for Marx, "shows that circumstances make men
just as much as men make circumstances [GI 59]."[64] And
it explicates the process in which men/women and circumstances create each other.

Engels addresses the question of consciousness,
freedom, and will in Anti-Duhring:

Hegel was the first to state correctly the
relation between freedom and necessity. To
him, freedom is the appreciation of necessity.
"Necessity is blind only in so far as it is not
understood." Freedom does not consist in the
dream of independence of natural laws, but in
the knowledge of these laws, and in the possibility this gives of systematically making them
work towards definite ends. This holds good in
relation both to the laws of external nature
and to those which govern the bodily and mental
existence of men themselves--two classes of
laws which we can separate from each other at
most only in thought but not in reality. Freedom of the will therefore means nothing but the
capacity to make decisions with real knowledge
of the subject.[65]

This issue is also addressed at length by Lenin.
In brief his position is this:

> Matter is primary, and thought, consciousness, sensation are products of a very high development. Such is the materialist theory of knowledge, to which natural science instinctively prescribes.[66]

Karl Korsch argues that Marx and Engels did not have a "dualistic metaphysical conception of the relationship of consciousness to reality."[67] His argument is that Marx and Engels were concerned with revolutionary change of material relations of production which "are what they are in combination with the forms in which they are reflected in the . . . consciousness of the period; and [the material relations] could not subsist in reality without these forms of consciousness."[68] He continues:

> Setting aside any philosophical considerations, it is therefore clear that without this coincidence of consciousness and reality, a critique of political economy could never become the major component of a theory of social revolution.[69]

As persistent as Marx is that ideas and consciousness, as such, do not create human history, he is equally sure that nature does not create that history. Who or what then has created and is creating modern human history? For Marxist theory, human history is created by intelligent, conscious human persons; persons who are at once social and species-beings and individuals. Marx writes:

> Nature builds no machines, no locomotives, railways, electric telegraphs, self-acting mules, etc. These are products of human industry; natural material transformed into organs of the human will over nature, or of human participation in nature. They are <u>organs of the human brain</u>, <u>created by the human hand</u>; the power of knowledge, objectified. The development of fixed capital indicates to what degree general social knowledge has become a <u>direct force of production</u>, and to what degree, hence, the conditions of the process of social life itself have come under the control of the general intellect and been transformed in accordance with it [<u>Grundrisse</u> 706].[70]

This statement is consistent with Marx's labor theory of value in <u>Capital</u> and with his position in 1844.[71] But more importantly it places the intellectual, conscious, willing human in the center of the process of <u>human</u> history.

It is one of the characteristics of the "School of Budapest," which includes, for example Lukacs, Gramsci, Korsch and Gyorgy Markus, to give forceful expression to this idea in Marx that it is human beings by their own activity who create themselves as human beings and, as such, create their own history.[72] Their emphasis, at this point, is that:

> Human beings and their history are therefore not fatalistically subject to abstract and general laws which exist above concrete struggles among individuals and groups of individuals; it is these struggles which, in the last instance, decide the direction of social change. This idea . . . is expressed today by the School of Budapest in such words as these of Gyorgy Markus: ". . . . The human being is a 'responsive being'--to use the words of Lukacs--who always reacts to the alternatives created by social development, and who is capable of transforming its spontaneously contradictory tendencies into questions the answers to which he or she consciously seeks."[73]

Gramsci accentuates this point when he writes:

> The individual does not enter into relations with other men by juxtaposition, but organically, in as much, that is, as he belongs to organic entities which range from the simplest to the most complex. Thus Man does not enter into relations with the natural world just by being himself part of the natural world, but actively, by means of work and technique. Further: these relations are not mechanical. They are active and conscious. They correspond to the greater or lesser degree of understanding that each man has of them. So one could say that each one of us changes himself, modifies himself to the extent that he changes and modifies the complex relations of which he is the hub.[74]

Human activity, informed by the general knowledge of the human intellect and directed by human will, is creating human society and history.[75] Marx is clear that human will is limited by (i) actual material conditions and (ii) knowledge of the nature of the human historical process.[76]

For Marx, knowledge and will do not of themselves actualize change in human society. Conscious awareness, however, sometimes can appear further advanced than the contemporary empirical relations (GI 88). This is because persons can consciously transcend their empirical existence. For example, in the German Ideology Marx refers to the many persons from other than the proletariat class who may gain consciousness of the need for revolution "through the contemplation of the situation" of the proletariat class (GI 94). In his earlier writing he makes reference to the ideas to which the French Revolution gave rise, which led beyond the ideas of the old world system; these ideas of course generated by humans (HF 160). And in the preface to Capital he refers to the significance of productive relations in relationship to the human capacity subjectively to rise above them (Capital I 10). In each of these cases there is a presupposed awareness of the human capacity to transcend consciously and understand existence, and to theorize about what should or might be. Marx combines this in each case with his theoretical position that conscious knowledge and the development of new ideas in themselves do not change existence.[77] Thus we can understand his criticism of Proudhon when Marx writes:

> You will now understand why M. Proudhon is the declared enemy of every political movement. The solution of present problems does not lie for him in public action but in the dialectical rotations of his own mind. Since to him the categories are the motive force, it is not necessary to change practical life in order to change the categories. Quite the contrary. [For Proudhon] one must change the categories and the consequence will be a change in the existing society [PP 191].[78]

For Marx, subjective human freedom is at once a matter of knowledge and material (inclusive of political) conditions; this is the essence of his discussion in the Holy Family (pp. 127ff), in which he writes, "The first proposition of profane socialism rejects emancipation in mere theory as an illusion and for real freedom it demands besides the idealistic will quite palpable material conditions [HF 127]." This is what he means when he speaks of "human emancipation" (HF 128).

Emancipation is emancipation from an alienating existence which for Marx is an existence in which human will is repressed. In the "First Manuscript" he writes:

90

The animal is one with its life activity. It does not distinguish the activity from itself. It is _its_ _activity_. But man makes his life activity itself an object of his will and consciousness. He has a conscious life activity. . . . Only for this reason is he a species-being. Or rather, he is only a self-conscious being, i.e. his own life is an object for him, because he is a species-being. Only for this reason is his activity free activity. Alienated labour reverses the relationship, in that man because he is a self-conscious being makes his life activity, his _being_, only a means for his _existence_.

The practical construction of an _objective_ _world_, the _manipulation_ of inorganic nature, is the confirmation of man as a conscious species-being, i.e. a being who treats the species as his own being or himself as a species-being. . . .

. . . .
Just as alienated labour transforms free and self-directed activity into a means, so it transforms the species-life of man into a means of physical existence [EPM 127-28].

In this statement Marx states that an aspect of what it means to be human is to make one's life activity itself an object of one's will and consciousness.[80] Species-being thus means not only membership in the human species, but the capacity of self-objectification or self-transcendence. This is an aspect of Marx's theory which must not read as an advocacy of individual freedom as such,[81] but a statement which argues that for humans to be human they must be free to do what they need to do and to have access to what they need, in order to develop their individual selves as species-beings. Marx writes:

The object of labour, is therefore, the _objectification_ of _man's_ _species-life_; for he no longer reproduces himself merely intellectually, as in consciousness, but actively and in a real sense, and he sees his own reflection in a world which he has constructed [EPM 128].

. . . he [the capitalist] ruthlessly forces the human race to produce for production's sake; he thus forces the development of the productive powers of society, and creates those material conditions, which alone can form the real basis

of a higher form of society, a society in which
the full and free development of every individual forms the ruling principle [Capital I
592].

I will discuss human freedom and development in
detail later in this chapter; the important point here is
to have demonstrated the central place of human activity
and subjective will in the context of socialist materialism.[82]

B. Consciousness at the Point
between Existence and Possibility

1. The Capacity to Make Judgments
and to Theorize

Without doubt, the most significant and convincing
evidence from Marx that humans have the capacity to make
conscious judgments and to theorize about the nature of
the past, the present and the possibilities for the future
are his own writings. With that point made I turn to the
content of the writings.

Marx formally introduces his method for doing research and theory in the German Ideology, even though we
will see it was already formed in his 1844 writings.   I
noted earlier that Marx begins with two basic assumptions;
(i) that there is a real world and (ii) all experience and
knowledge of the world comes to us through our senses.[83]
With this in mind we can turn to the German Ideology where
Marx writes:

First Premises of Materialist Method
The premises from which we begin are not arbitrary ones, not dogmas, but real premises from
which   abstraction can only be made in the
imagination. They are the real individuals,
their activity and the material conditions under which they live, both those which they find
already existing and those produced by their
activity. These premises can thus be verified
in a purely empirical way.
The first premise of all human history is,
of course, the existence of living human individuals. Thus the first fact to be established
is the physical organization of these individuals and their consequent relation to the
rest of nature. . . . geological, oreohydro-
graphical, climatic and so on. The writing of

history must always set out from these natural bases and their modification in the course of history through the action of men [GI 42].

Marx does not deal with a metaphysical philosophical ontological analysis (as Whitehead does) of how it is that the thought process emerges. However, he does begin at exactly the same place as Whitehead, i.e., with the real sensuous human persons who find themselves (Grundrisse 490) within a real world, from which abstractions can only be made in the mind or imagination. This is the process of thinking (Grundrisse 101), reflecting and imagining abstractly about the real world.[84] Not only do humans find themselves in material and social conditions, they find that these material and social (and cultural) conditions have been created by humans. These premises, according to Marx, can be verified empirically (GI 46-48).[85] We noted earlier the five points of Marx's developed theory. First, humans must live to make history. Second, humans create new needs when they create instruments to satisfy present needs. Third, human production-reproduction becomes a social process with institutionalized social relations. Four, human productive-reproductive history thus has a dual nature, i.e., material and social. And five, it is in this material and social productive-reproductive process that human consciousness and language emerge. Thus in any discussion of humans theorizing, at the point between present existence and future possibility, existence can be defined as (i) the definite material conditions, (ii) the definite forms of activity or modes of living, and (iii) the definite culture or belief systems. Marx explains the relationship of these three variables and his materialist concept of history this way:

> This conception of history depends on our ability to expound the real process of production, starting out from the material production of life itself, and to comprehend the form of intercourse connected with this and created by this mode of production (i.e. civil society in its various stages), as the basis of all history; and to show it in its action as State, to explain all the different theoretical products and forms of consciousness, religion, philosophy, ethics, etc. and trace their origins and growth from the basis; by which means, of course, the whole thing can be depicted in its totality (and therefore, too, the reciprocal action of these various sides on one another). It is not, like the idealistic view of history, in every period to look for a category, but

remains constantly on the real ground of history; it does not explain practice from the idea but explains the formation of ideas from material practice; . . . [GI 58, my emphasis].

It must be remembered that Marx's work, in addition to analyzing capitalism, was a critical response to idealism;[86] nonetheless, here in his critique of German idealist philosophy we find the three key variables, viz., (i) material reality, (ii) forms of relations or intercourse and (iii) forms of consciousness; plus the affirmation of their reciprocal action on one another.[87]

In this view of history the capacity to theorize is always in the context and limits of the given and structured material, social and cultural conditions, that is to say, in the context of "actual" history (GI 48). This is why Marx claims that:

Mankind thus inevitably sets itself only such tasks as it is able to solve, since closer examination will always show that the problem itself arises only when the material conditions for its solution are already present or at least in the course of formation [Critique 21].

That is to say, consciousness is always grounded in reality, and even (as we noted in both Marx and Whitehead) abstract theoretical conceptual possibilities find their origin in references to real history.[88]

It is in the Grundrisse, in his discussion of capital, that Marx in a few lines sets down the logic as to how an empirical understanding of the present points toward an understanding of the past, how the present emerges out of the past, and how this combined knowledge enables humans to theorize about, or have "foreshadowings of the future." He writes:

. . . the correct observation and deduction of these laws, [of bourgeois economy] as having themselves become[55] in history, always leads to primary equations - like the empirical numbers e.g. in natural science - which point towards a past lying behind this system. These indications [Andeutung], together with a correct grasp of the present, then also offer the key to the understanding of the past . . . This correct view likewise leads at the same time to the points at which the suspension of the present form of production relations gives signs of its becoming - foreshadowings of the future [Grundrisse 460-61].

---

[55]Having themselves become = having themselves undergone the process of becoming, as indicated on pp. 459-60.

Knowledge of the past and present derived empirically via the senses is thus the content with which persons theorize. This is also the theoretical position maintained by Mao Tse-Tung:

> With the continuation of man's social practice, the sensations and images of a thing are repeated innumerable times, and then a sudden change in the cognitive process takes place, resulting in the formation of concepts. Concepts as such no longer represent the external aspects of things, their individual aspects, or their external relations. Through concepts man comes to grasp a thing in its entirety, its essence, and its internal relations. Conception is not only quantitatively but also qualitatively different from perception. . . . This is the second stage of knowledge. . . . In the complete process of knowing a thing, this stage of conception, judgment, and inference is more important than the first stage. It is the stage of rational knowledge. The real task of cognition is to arrive at thought through perception, at a gradual understanding of the internal contradictions of objective things, their laws, the internal relations between this and that process, that is, a rational knowledge . . .[89]

It is important to emphasize this empirical-sense basis for theorizing because for Marx, theorizing never takes place in pure abstraction, but rather always in some way related to sense experience of reality; Marx speaks of the "senses" having become "directly theoreticians in practice" (EPM 160). The senses are the means by which persons become-one-with and know the world around them. Marx writes:

> . . . the senses and minds of other men have become my own appropriation. Thus besides these direct organs, social organs are constituted, in the form of society; for example, activity in direct association with others has

become an organ for the manifestation of life
and a mode of appropriation of human life [EPM
160].

Marx is not concerned with the human capacity to make
judgments or to theorize, as such, in the abstract. Thus
his statements which deal with this capacity, i.e., to
theorize consciously, are usually in terms of some particular person or groups, e.g., socialists, bourgeoisie,
or proletarians, theorizing in a particular historical
context. Nor does he ever lose sight of limits he places
upon theorizing, which I noted above when I quoted his
statement to the effect that solutions to problems confronted have material conditions existent or in formation
for their solution. Putting together his notions of (i)
a real world empirically understood via the senses and
(ii) the necessary historical situation for productive
theorizing; this is what he writes about socialist theorists:

> Socialism . . . begins from the theoretical and
> practical sense perception of man and nature as
> essential beings [EPM 167].

> . . . the Socialists and the Communists are the
> theoreticians of the proletarian class. So
> long as the proletariat is not yet sufficiently
> developed to constitute itself as a class, and
> consequently so long as the struggle itself of
> the proletariat with the bourgeoisie has not
> yet assumed a political character, and the
> productive forces are not yet sufficiently de-
> veloped in the bosom of the bourgeoisie itself
> to enable us to catch a glimpse of the material
> conditions necessary for the emancipation of
> the proletariat and for the formation of a new
> society, these theoreticians are merely
> utopians who, to meet the wants of the oppres-
> sed classes, improvise systems and go in search
> of a regenerating science. But in the measure
> that history moves forward, and with it the
> struggle of the proletariat assumes clearer
> outlines, they no longer need to seek science
> in their minds; they have only to take note of
> what is happening before their eyes and to be-
> come its mouthpiece [PP 125].

We see in these and the references in the earlier
sections of this chapter, not only the human capacity to
be conscious, to think and to theorize; but also we see

that, for Marx, any theorizing, to be of significance for the historical process, must not simply be mental system building, but must struggle conceptually with actual people in their actual situations.[90] To be the "mouth piece" of "what is happening" is not as benign as it might appear. This is because when theoretical descriptions of their exploited condition and the awareness of the centralness of persons and human labor in the creation of history are brought to the conscious awareness of the proletariat, this theory becomes a powerful motivating force, thus legitimizing the theorizing activity. Marx writes:

> . . . theory itself becomes a material force when it has seized the masses. Theory is capable of seizing the masses when it demonstrates ad hominem, and it demonstrates ad hominem as soon as it becomes radical. To be radical is to grasp things by the root. But for man the root is man himself [CHR 52].[91]

Theorizing gains this significance by accurately describing the nature and process of actual human productive and reproductive processes ad hominem, i.e., in terms of human interests,[92] and discrediting or stripping away the existing conceptual schemes which mask both the true character of actual economic and social processes and the fact that persons are the creators and the ends of history. This second process is exemplified in Marx's discussion of the criticism of religion, as well as in his criticism of capitalist categories in the Grundrisse and Capital (especially in the demystification of money, and the origin of value as other than human labor).

Note this passage on the criticism of religion as an example of Marx's understanding of the importance of the task of critical theory in stripping away falsehood and revealing the human task of humanizing the world:

> Criticism has plucked the imaginary flowers from the chain, not in order that man shall bear the chain without caprice or consolation but so that he shall cast off the chain and pluck the living flower. The criticism of religion disillusions man so that he will think, act and fashion his reality as a man who has lost his illusions and regained his reason; so that he will revolve about himself as his own true sun.
> . . .

It is the task of history, therefore, once the other-world of truth has vanished, to establish the truth of this world [CHR 44].

The unmasking, enabling criticism does not stop with religion. That task, Marx assumed, had been effectively accomplished by Feuerbach.[93] Thus Marx writes that the "immediate task of philosophy, which is in the service of history, is to unmask human self-alienation in its secular form . . . [CHR 44]."[94] Thus the criticism is now focused on the "earth," "law" and "politics" (CHR 44). In this context Lenin writes:

> The highest task of humanity is to comprehend the objective logic of economic evolution (the evolution of social life) in its general and fundamental features, so that it may be possible to adapt to it one's social consciousness and the consciousness of the advanced classes of all capitalist countries in as definite, clear and critical a fashion as possible.[95]

Thus, for Marx, the human capacity to make judgments and to theorize is a capacity with which sensuous humans find themselves. However in order for that capacity to be relevant for conscious human intervention in the historical process, the conscious theorizing person must (i) theorize out of close sensuous empirical contact with the real world,[96] and (ii) within the context of the accumulated empirical knowledge of this world in natural and human science.[97] As Korsch notes, for Marx:

> Intellectual life should be conceived in union with social and political life, and social being and becoming (in the widest sense, as economics, politics or law) should be studied in union with social consciousness in its many different manifestations, as a real yet also ideal (or 'ideological') component of the historical process in general.[98]

We see here in Marx and Korsch the implicit framework of praxis, i.e., theory and empirical practice in a reciprocally informing process,[99] which I will discuss in greater detail later in the chapter.

2. The Capacity to Judge Types of Economic, Social and Cultural Existence for Their Capacity to Enable Human Development

One does not have to read long in Marx's writings before it is very clear that Marx is not only describing the origin and development of human history but he also is doing normative criticism of the capitalist mode of production and its corresponding culture. Beyond the criticism Marx is both predicting and advocating revolutionary change in the mode of production and the whole corresponding socio-political structure and culture. In the present study I am concerned with the human capacity to intervene in the process of human history. In my discussion of Whitehead I noted that the social nature of reality, including persons, and the experiential character of the individual subject had defining and limiting implications for effective conscious intervention in the historical process. So in like manner with Marx; it is important to understand both the given (sensuously and empirically discovered) characteristics of reality, including persons, and the capacity to discern which economic, social and cultural realities are most compatible with, and facilitative of, the development of human persons. Thus it is appropriate for Ollman to write, in his discussion on whether or not there is a Marxian ethic:

> He (Marx) never, however, goes beyond stating the relations involved when he himself approves or condemns anything, or when he concludes from a situation what must be done. It is no coincidence that other thinkers who possess a philosophy of internal relations--Spinoza, Leibniz, Hegel, Dietzgen, etc.--have likewise foresworn the fact-value distinction; for partaking of this philosophical tradition any value judgment would have to be understood as internally related to what they know, and hence as an expression of all that makes it both possible and necessary.[100]

Gramsci writes that the genesis of the "philosophy of praxis," i.e., Marxism, is "'materialism' perfected by the work of speculative philosophy itself and fused with humanism."[101] Althusser provides the Marxist qualification of Gramsci's statement with his criticism of idealistic or socialistic "humanism" as a dogma, theory or ethic which describes the essence of humans.[102] He however does radically affirm the necessity and the human capacity to be theoretical and to develop theory. In this context he seems to affirm the use of "human development" as an _empirically_ discerned theoretical referent, which is not external to history, and is only directional as is other emergent theory in "theory practice."[103] His criticism of "humanism" is not anti-human or anti-person; it is a classic Marxist warning that only doing ethics, or theoretically discerning the essence of humans without actualizing material changes, will not solve real problems.

> Simply put, the recourse to ethics so deeply inscribed in every humanist ideology may play the part of an imaginary treatment of real problems. Once _known_, these problems are posed in precise terms; they are organizational problems of the forms of economic life, political life, and individual life. To pose these problems correctly and to resolve them in reality, they must be called by their names, _their scientific_ names. The slogan of humanism has no theoretical value, but it does have value as a practical index: we must get down to the concrete problems themselves, that is, to their knowledge, if we are to produce the historical transformation whose necessity was thought by Marx.[104]

This is an important warning to be kept in mind whenever one begins a discussion of the normative characteristic of Marx's writings. Engels presents a lengthy criticism of "morality" and ethics.[105] His analysis concludes that morality is historical, and that as long as there are classes there will be "class morality."[106]

Engels does not argue against making normative judgments and decisions. He argues that we must historicize "ethics." He concludes that a "really human morality which transcends class antagonisms and their legacies in thought becomes possible only at a stage of society which has not only overcome class contradictions but has even forgotten them in practical life."[107] "Really human" is a recurrent concept in Marx. It is however not an external or finished human nature.[108] Gramsci makes this point when he writies that there is no abstract "human nature," fixed and immutable, but that "human nature is a totality of historically determined social relations, hence _an historical fact which can_, within certain limits, _be ascertained_ with the methods of philology and criticism."[109] It may be helpful to recall, from Chapter I, the distinction between real and actual. The comments by Engels and Gramsci can be understood to mean that a historical really human morality can, within limits, be ascertained through conscious philology, criticism and--as I will discuss in detail later--praxis. This historically ascertained human nature or really human morality is real in two ways, viz., it is conceptually real and it is potentially real in present actual history. But it is not possible for it to be actual until the material-structural-cultural society changes and overcomes actual class contradictions. For Marxist theory, what is really human is not eternal but historical. This does not mean that the really human is not enduring or persistent. For Marxist theory, what Marcuse writes about "truth"[110] applies also to human nature. That is to say, human nature transcends the given historical reality, but only in so far as it crosses from one historical stage to another. We can gain understanding of this perspective by analogy from historical--but enduring--human anatomical structures. Again by analogy, the really human morality is, within limits, ascertained in present society in much the same way that physical health is, within limits, ascertained through observation, theory and practical activity in relation to "sick" and "healthy" people. This process or method in Marxist theory and medicine is the ascertaining of the historical <u>ought</u> from the historical <u>is</u>.

Ollman confuses the issue when he writes: "Contrary to a widely accepted opinion, Marx has . . . a conception of man 'outside of history'."[111] What he--Ollman--means is that Marx has a conception of "human nature in general" and of "what is common to all men at all times."[112] The categories he discusses in this context are the natural and species human powers, needs, potentials, and capacities. What Ollman fails to emphasize--or perhaps realize--is that these categories do not, as Marx used them, place human nature "outside of history." Nonetheless Ollman's study of Marx's theory confirms the importance of human development for Marxist theory, which we describe in this chapter.[113]

Marx is not systematic in his explication of reality, but there are at least four important characteristics of natural and human reality which are explicitly recurrent and constantly implicit in all of his writings, which reveal his understanding of the nature of reality, and his assumption that what is desired is the actualization of the potential in nature. First, I have already noted that Marx claims sensuous, empirical, practically tested, and critical research as a basis for his conclusions as to the nature of reality. I have also noted these other characteristics separately; but I note them here together to demonstrate what Marx considers the objective normative referent for his political economic analysis. Second, for Marx, the character of nature inclusive of humanity is organically social. I discussed this at length in the first section of this chapter. Third, Marx understands the nature of humans to be species-being. This characteristic of humans has two sub-characteristics: (a) humans are uniquely internally and externally related to their fellow humans, this is most obviously seen in their interdependent productive relations where each individual is at once a means for others and an end in him/herself, and (b) humans have the unique capacity to be self-conscious in their labor and activity, i.e., they can be self-transcendent of themselves. And fourth, the locus of value seems clearly to be in the development of, or actualization of, the human persons as physical and mental species-individuals; and subsequently "use value" is more than a descriptive term, i.e., it becomes in many cases a positive reference to that which can be used for human development.[114] The social and species-character of humans is discussed earlier in the chapter. However, the notion that the locus of value is the human person and that the normative referent is the goal of actualization of human potential or human development deserves more discussion and documentation.

Marx discusses human development as the <u>end</u> and <u>reason</u> of human history in the <u>German Ideology</u>, reaffirms it strongly in the <u>Grundrisse</u>, and makes it explicit in <u>Capital</u>,[115] and also in 1875 in the <u>Critique of the Gotha Program</u>.[116] I will now discuss these references.

In the first passage which I will quote from <u>German Ideology</u>, Marx is concerned with the development of the many-sides (physical and mental) or capacities of the human individual.[117] He is also very clear that the development, or crippling, of these qualities or capacities is directly dependent upon the varied activities and practical relations in which the individual live. The obvious implication is that full human development is compatible with only certain types of activity and empirical practical relations. The importance and material context of thought are also made explicit. Marx writes:

> If the circumstances in which the individual lives allow him only the [one]-sided development of a single quality at the expense of all the rest, if they give him the material and time to develop only that one quality, then this individual achieves only a <u>one-sided</u>, <u>crippled</u>

development.* No moral preaching avails here. And the manner in which this one, preferentially favored quality develops depends again, on the one hand, on the material available for its development and, on the other hand, on the degree and manner in which the other qualities are suppressed. . . .

In the case of an individual, for example, whose life embraces a wide circle of varied activities and practical relations to the world, and who, therefore, lives a many-sided life, thought has the same character of universality as every other manifestation of his life. Consequently, it neither becomes fixed in the form of abstract thought nor does it need complicated tricks of reflection when the individual passes from thought to some other manifestation of life. From the outset it is always a factor in the total life of the individual, one which disappears and is reproduced as required . . .

The fact that under favorable circumstances some individuals are able to rid themselves of their local narrow-mindedness is . . . because they, in their empirical reality, and owing to empirical needs, have been able to bring about world intercourse [GI 105-06, *my emphasis].

We note within the above quotation, not only emphasis on many-sided development, but also a reference to the reciprocity between thought and the other manifestations (activity or practice) of life.

In a later section of German Ideology Marx discusses the free development of the individual in the context of criticism of private property. His point is that productive forces and forms of intercourse have made possible, and are a prerequisite for, a fully developed human, but the "all-round development of individuals" will not be possible in the context of private property as a socioeconomic form. He argues that it will be only in a communist socio-economic structure that the desired "free development of individuals" can be actualized. This is in no sense an affirmation of individualism but rather a materialist argument for the socio-economic conditions which will enable the full development of species-individuals. Marx writes:

. . . private property can be abolished only on condition of an all-round development of in-

dividuals, because the existing character of
intercourse and productive forces is an all-
round one, and only individuals that are developing in an all-round fashion can appropriate them, i.e. can turn them into free
manifestations of their lives. We have shown
that at the present time individuals must
abolish private property, because the productive forces and forms of intercourse have developed so far that, under the domination of
private property, they have become destructive
forces, and because the contradiction between
the classes has reached its extreme limit.
. . .
Within communist society, the only society in
which the original and free development of individuals ceases to be a mere phrase, this development is determined precisely by the connection of individuals, a connection which
consists [i] partly in the economic prerequisites and [ii] partly in the necessary soli-
darity of the free development of all, and, finally, [iii] in the universal character of the
activity of individuals on the basis of the
existing productive forces [GI 117-18, my em-
phasis].

In the above quotation Marx not only affirms (i) human
development as the goal, and (ii) the capitalist development of facilitating forces of production; but he goes on
to say that capitalist forms of production and intercourse, i.e., private property[118] and individualism, are
incompatible with further free development of species-
individuals. This understanding is present also in the
"Communist Manifesto," where Marx and Engels write: "In
place of the old bourgeois society, with its classes and
class antagonisms, we shall have an association in which
the free development of each is the condition for the free
development of all."[119]

It is probable that Marx's richest and most con-
centrated affirmation of the development of human capacities as the empirically discerned normative reference
for human society is found in the center of the Grundrisse.[120] It is in the form of a long rhetorical
question. He writes:

In fact, however, when the limited bourgeois
form is stripped away, what is wealth other
than [i] the universality of individual needs,

104

capacities, pleasures, productive forces, etc., created through universal exchange? [ii] The full development of human mastery over the forces of nature, those of so-called nature as well as of humanity's own nature? [iii] The absolute working-out of his creative potentialities, with no presupposition other than the previous historic development, which makes this totality of development, i.e. the development of all human powers as such the end in itself, not as measured on a predetermined yardstick? [iv] Where he does not reproduce himself in one specificity, but produces his totality? [and (v) Where he/she] strives not to remain something he has become, but is in the absolute movement of becoming? In bourgeois economics --and in the epoch of production to which it corresponds--this complete working-out of the human content appears as a complete emptying-out, this universal objectification as total alienation, and the tearing-down of all limited, one-sided aims as sacrifice of the human end-in-itself to an entirely external end [Grundrisse 488].

For Marx, in this passage, the human is an end-in-itself, but not a thing-in-itself, that is to say, wealth and value rest in "becoming," "development," "producing" and in "working-out of creative potentialities." Wealth and value for Marx are clearly in men/women's active self-creation of their individual species-being.

This is also an appropriate place to refer again to Marx's reference in Capital to the higher form of society which is being made possible by the development of greater and more efficient forces of production: ". . . a society in which the full and free development of every individual forms the ruling principle [Capital I 592]." This is probably a reference to a high phase of communist society;[121] a society which Korsch anticipates thus:

Not until that phase of the communist society of the future, . . . when labour will have developed from being a means of living to a spontaneous activity of man and, along with a development of all creative powers of the human individual the productive forces of society will also have increased; not till all springs of cooperative wealth are in full flow--not until then will the inhuman sacrifice of the

105

present for the future of society become super-
fluous and the single-track idea of "progress"
branch out into the universal development of
free individuals in a free society.[122]

Marx also associates the primacy of human development with a communist society in his 1846 German Ideology
and in his 1875 Critique of the Gotha Programme. In this
later work we read:

> In a higher phase of communist society, after
> the enslaving subordination of individuals un-
> der division of labour, and therewith also the
> antithesis between mental and physical labour,
> has vanished; after labour, from a mere means
> of life, has itself become the prime necessity
> of life; after the productive forces have also
> increased with the all-round development of the
> individual, and all the springs of cooperative
> wealth flow more abundantly—only then can the
> narrow horizon of bourgeois right be fully left
> behind and society inscribe on its banners:
> from each according to his ability, to each
> according to his needs! [CGP 10, my emphasis].

When Marx makes such a statement about human development
as a goal, it is always set in the context of (i) adequate
material forces of production, (ii) economic and social
relations which are compatible with species-ness (in its
dual aspect), and (iii) access to what is necessary for the
actualization or development of human powers and capacities.

It is because human development (and derivatively
forces and relations of production) is so central in Marx,
that labor and labor-created use value gain central importance. That is to say, use value is by definition that
which has utility in the actualization and development of
species-individuals.[123] Marx writes in the Grundrisse:
"use value is not concerned with human activity as the
source of the product, with its having been posited by
human activity, but with its being for mankind [Grundrisse
613, my emphasis]." Or in his discussion of commodities
in Capital, Marx writes essentially the same thing, while
giving credit to human labor and to "mother earth," he
writes:

> So far therefore as labour is a creator of use-
> value, is useful labour, it is a necessary
> condition, independent of all forms of society,

> for the existence of the human race; it is an
> eternal nature-imposed necessity, without
> which there can be no material exchanges be-
> tween man and Nature, and therefore no life.
> . . . We see, then, that labour is not the only
> source of material wealth, of use-values pro-
> duced by labour. As William Petty puts it,
> labour is its father and the earth its mother
> [Capital I 42-43].

Human labor is the father and the earth is the mother of
use value, and the end of use value is humanity, itself,
as Marx writes when he quotes Galiani:

> About use value, Galiani nicely says: 'Price
> is a relation . . . the price of things is their
> proportion relative to our need*, which has as
> yet no fixed measure. But this will be found.
> I myself believe it to be man himself.' . . .
> 'It is, rather, he' (man) 'who is the sole and
> true wealth.' . . . [Grundrisse 847, *my empha-
> sis].

When reading the last sentence of this quotation, it is
appropriate to understand the term "wealth" in terms of
the long quotation given above from the Grundrisse, p.
488.

Thus it is clear that if (i) the earth, i.e., nature
is the mother, (ii) human labor is the father, i.e.,
creator, and (iii) developed, actualized, species-individuals can only develop or actualize their powers and
capacities under certain types of material, and socially
structured conditions, then it becomes of paramount importance for humans who wish to intervene creatively and
consciously in the historical process to facilitate that
human development to be able to discern which material,
structural and cultural conditions are compatible with
such human development.[124] The question can be asked:
Does Marx provide any clues as to whether or not, and how
conscious humans can make these judgments?

It can be said that Marx's life work is testimony to
the fact that he assumed humans could make these judgments
of compatibility (relative to actual situations and progressively as history emerges), but there is little if any
evidence that Marx (i) either thought he foresaw how a
final human society would be structured, or (ii) that he
posited that there would be a final human society; particularly the Grundrisse demonstrates that Marx viewed

107

human society and human history as an ongoing process.[125] Marx's work on alienation and his criticism of capital, however, are judgments of the incompatibility of some existing economic, structural and cultural conditions, with human development; and by inference they (along with his reference to socialism and communism) point in a direction toward which Marx believed human society will move as the mode of production changes and must move if it is to become a more human society.

Marx studied philosophy, human history, and economic, political and social theory. Beyond that he observed first hand the working, production, and living conditions of workers in England and western Europe. In his own study and reflection, Marx was aided particularly by the development of natural and industrial science, and by Feuerbach's critique of theism, i.e., Feuerbach's materialism.[126] Marx came to what he considered an empirically based and rationally sound conclusion as to (i) the social and materialist character of nature and human reality and (ii) the human creation of human history by species-individuals. As Korsch notes:

> Hegel started from the "idea." Marx, on the contrary, in all his philosophical, juridical, and political studies took his start from a strictly empirical principle. He approached the historical, social, and practical world of man with the firm decision to investigate this so-called "world of the mind" which until then had been treated as something essentially different from physical and material nature, with the same "precision" which has been applied for several centuries by the great scientists to their study of physical nature.[127]

For Marx, his own experiences, the productive and social situation and the above conclusions were not his private domain, but were public reality. It was a public fact that natural science had already demonstrated the human capacity to direct and organize, rationally and intellectually (with the aid of accumulated knowledge), the productive practice and social existence.[128] Given the public facts and a little "free time"[129] for reflection on past practice and existence, and the situation is ripe for the process of judging the compatibility of certain types of present and potential productive, social and cultural forms, with the development of human species-individuals.

The next question is, to what extent can humans actualize in human history the implications of their judgments and conscious intentions?

3. The Capacity to Influence the Present and Future

The contemporary category which describes the process (as Marx understood it) by which humans consciously influence their present and future historical existence is "praxis." This, however, as a category of Marx's, is not the formal process of revolutionary praxis as developed theoretically by Mao Tse-tung. The last sentence of Mao's essay "On Practice," reads:

> The discovery of truths through practice, the verification and the development of them through practice, the active development of perceptual knowledge into rational knowledge and, by means of rational knowledge, the active direction of revolutionary practice and the reconstruction of the subjective and the external world-practice, knowledge, more practice, more knowledge, and the repetition ad infinitum of this cyclic pattern, and with each cycle, the elevation of the content of practice and knowledge to a higher level--such is the epistemology of dialectical materialism, such is its theory of the unity of knowledge and action.[130]

Marx is, however, considered a praxis theoretician by most Marxists, including such men as Lenin, George Lukacs,[131] Antonio Gramsci, Jurgen Habermas[132] and Louis Althusser.[133] Gramsci, in 1932, writes of how Ricardo's theories of economics encouraged "the first theoreticians of the philosophy of praxis to go beyond Hegel's philosophy in order to construct a new historicism uncontaminated by vestiges of speculative logic."[134] The "first theoreticians of the philosophy of praxis" obviously refers to Marx and Engels. But until Mao developed praxis as a revolutionary, ongoing process, praxis often meant simply that consciousness and self-consciousness, and thus theory or philosophy, were grounded in and informed by existence, and that the accuracy of any conceptual or theoretical statement must be tested, i.e., verified, in practice or actual sense experience. Lenin's emphasis on "verification" is a good example of this.[135] However it must be noted that there are exceptions such as Korsch[136] and Gramsci. Gramsci, for example, writes:

> If the problem of the identification of theory and practice is to be raised, it can be done in this sense, that one can construct, on a specific practice, a theory which, by coinciding and identifying itself with the decisive elements of the practice itself, can accelerate the historical process that is going on, rendering practice more homogeneous, more coherent, more efficient in all its elements, and thus, in other words, developing its potential to the maximum: or alternatively, given a certain theoretical position one can organise the practical element which is essential for the theory to be realised. The identification of theory and practice is a critical act, through which practice is demonstrated rational and necessary, and theory realistic and rational.[137]

The closest approximation to a developed concept of praxis in Marx is in the first three of his well known Theses on Feuerbach. In the first thesis he criticizes Feuerbach for not grasping "the significance of 'revolutionary,' 'practical-critical' activity."[138] In the second he writes: "Man must prove the truth, i.e. the reality and power, the 'this-sidedness' of his thinking in practice [TF 67]."[139] And in the third he writes:

> The materialist doctrine concerning the changing of circumstances and education forgets that circumstances are changed by men, and that the educator must himself be educated.
> . . .
> The coincidence of the changing of circumstances and of human activity or self-changing can only be grasped and rationally understood as revolutionary practice [TF 67 & 68].

This is, of course, a reference to Feuerbach's materialism, not to materialism as Marx understood it. Furthermore, "revolutionary practice," in this context means educated, theoretically informed practice. Marx in the above passage is criticizing what Mao calls "pre-Marxist materialism" when he writes:

> Pre-Marxist materialism (mechanistic materialism) did not stress the thought process in the development of knowledge, but regarded

> thought merely as the object of action, as the
> mirror that reflects nature. . . . Only dia-
> lectical materialism correctly shows the ac-
> tive role of thought, and at the same time
> points out the limitation imposed upon thought
> by matter. It points out that thought arises
> from social practice and at the same time ac-
> tively shapes practice.[140]

On first reading Lenin appears to be the kind of
materialist that Marx and Mao are criticizing, because
Lenin speaks of "consciousness which reflects nature and
the nature which is reflected by consciousness."[141] The
reason Lenin is not a pre-Marxist materialist is that the
issue for him is one of idealism versus materialism, and
not praxis versus mechanistic materialism. Lenin is not
a mechanistic materialist who denies the power of thought
or theory, but a dialectical materialist who affirms that
(i) the world is really out there, (ii) our perceptions and
ideas are a reflection of what is really external to us and
(iii) practice is the means by which we verify our images.
He writes:

> Thus the materialist theory, the theory of
> reflection of objects by our mind, is here
> presented with absolute clarity: things exist
> outside us. Our perceptions and ideas are
> their images. Verification of these images,
> differentiation between true and false images,
> is given by practice.[142]

In the Theses on Feuerbach, we find theory which is
close to contemporary "praxis" theory (as informed by
Mao); and if we look at several of Marx's earlier and later
writings we will find the fundamental elements of praxis
exist in his works from the Manuscripts through the third
volume of Capital. What is important is not that the
theory is consistently found throughout his writings,[143]
but that fundamental to Marx's materialist-economic
analysis there is a clearly defined affirmation of the
human capacity to theorize and to intervene consciously in
history, as well as a delineation of the limits of that
capacity. We will now look at the praxis motif in a number
of passages in Marx's writings so that we can more clearly
understand how, within a Marxist materialist scheme, it is
possible for species-individuals to intervene consciously
in the process of human history.

In the "Introduction" to his contribution to the
Critique of Hegel's Philosophy of Right, Marx speaks of

the importance of human criticism plucking the imaginary flowers from "the chain." Why? Not so that persons will continue to be oppressed in full knowledge of their exploitation and alienation, but so that by being informed the oppressed persons can act in the light of knowledge; i.e., critical theory enables a person to "think, act and fashion his reality as a man who has lost his illusions and regained his reason [CHR 44]." Remembering that, for Marx, theory or criticism is always informed by empirical, sensuous experience of what is, it is not difficult to find in this passage, criticism informed by existence and this informed criticism informing practice which in turn liberates further reasonable action. This is in fact the praxis cycle. This same point is made later in the same work when Marx links the "arm of criticism" with the "criticism of arms", which together end in the overthrow of those conditions "in which man is an abased, enslaved, abandoned, contemptible being [CHR 52]." Or again he writes: "Just as philosophy finds its material weapons in the proletariat, so the proletariat finds its intellectual weapons in philosophy [CHR 59]."

In the Manuscripts, Marx writes that socialism "begins from the theoretical and practical sense perception of man and nature as essential beings [EPM 167]." And furthermore, that these humans emerge from and in nature creating their own society and history. And it has come to pass that human society has developed "private property with its wealth and poverty (both intellectual and material), . . . [EPM 162]." The contradictions which exist in this society go beyond wealth and poverty; they are real, and they have theoretical expressions. The point which Marx goes on to make is that the theoretical contradictions are reflections of real contradictions, and though it is good and helpful that the real contradictions are given theoretical expression, it is false to assume that the contradictions can be solved with theory; at best theoretical expressions will illuminate real contradictions which can thus more easily be solved with practical activity. He writes:

> The resolution of the theoretical contradictions is possible only through practical means, only through the practical energy of man. Their resolution is not by any means, therefore, only a problem of knowledge, but is a real problem of life which philosophy was unable to solve precisely because it saw there a purely theoretical problem [EPM 162].

Marx is critical of knowledge and philosophy only when they become separated from the real activity and problems of human society.[144] Theoretical contradictions which reflect real contradictions, which can be solved only by real practical activity, are not only an expression of praxis, but provide the insight that conscious persons intervene in history via theoretically informed practical activity. This is also the position reiterated by Mao.[145]

Fundamental to Marx's understanding of theory and practice (which is almost always in the context of the development of liberation of human persons) is the assertion that serious praxis or liberation must <u>always</u> be in a situation which includes the developed material conditions for the actualization of that development or liberation; that is why he writes:

> . . . it is only possible to achieve real liberation in the real world and by employing real means, . . . slavery cannot be abolished without the steam-engine and the mule and spinning-jenny, serfdom cannot be abolished without improved agriculture, and . . . in general, people cannot be liberated as long as they are unable to obtain food and drink, housing and clothing in adequate quality and quantity. "Liberation" is an historical and not a mental act, and it is brought about by historical conditions, the development of industry, commerce, agriculture, the conditions of intercourse. . . . [GI 61].

I have included this quotation to illustrate the importance for Marx, of adequate <u>conditions</u> and developed <u>forces</u> of production. "Liberation," as used in the quotation, refers not only to political and ideological liberation, but to liberation from necessity.

Marx, in his discussions which imply praxis, in <u>German Ideology</u>, <u>Grundrisse</u> and <u>Capital</u>, assumes the social and species character of humans. He assumes that change should be rationally planned in the context of accumulated knowledge. Furthermore, this change should develop forces of production and communal structures which facilitate the free, conscious development of species-individuals. Thus the formal process of praxis is implicit, but not elaborated as such.

In the German Ideology he writes:

> . . . the liberation of each single individual
> will be accomplished in the measure in which
> history becomes transformed into world his-
> tory. From the above it is clear that the real
> intellectual wealth of the individual depends
> entirely on the wealth of his real connections.
> Only then will the separate individuals be
> liberated from the various national and local
> barriers, be brought into practical connection
> with the material and intellectual production
> of the whole world and be put in a position to
> acquire the capacity to enjoy this all-sided
> production of the whole earth (the creations of
> man). All-round dependence, this natural form
> of the world-historical co-operation of indi-
> viduals, will be transformed by this communist
> revolution into the control and conscious
> mastery* of these powers, which, born of the
> action of men on one another, have till now over
> awed and governed men as powers completely
> alien to them [GI 55, *my emphasis].

In the above quotation Marx is particularly concerned with
world-wide cooperative structuring of material and intellectual production. Why? Because real material and
intellectual liberation of individuals will come through
the practical activity of cooperation; and furthermore
that activity will enable further conscious mastery of
emerging productive powers. The quotation can be understood as a praxis statement only if it is remembered that
it is a theoretical statement (based on prior empirical-
practical observation), which calls for further practical
activity, which in turn will liberate increased intellectual wealth and conscious mastery. Marx making the
statement is an example of the theoretical side of the
dialectic of praxis.

Closer to the praxis motif; in the Grundrisse Marx
discusses communal production and the importance of planning. He theorizes that individuals and societies must
economize and plan their practical activity in such a way
as to give them time to achieve adequate knowledge (theory), which in turn will satisfy the demands of their
activity and development. He writes:

> On the basis of communal production, the
> determination of time remains, of course, es-
> sential. The less time the society requires to

produce wheat, cattle etc., the more time it
wins for other production, material or mental.
Just as in the case of an individual, the
multiplicity of its development, its enjoyment
and its activity depends on economization of
time. . . . [Society] just as the individual has
to distribute his time correctly in order to
satisfy the various demands on his activity.
Thus, economy of time, along with the planned
distribution of labour time among the various
branches of production [material and mental],
remains the first economic law on the basis of
communal production [Grundrisse 172-73, my em-
phasis].

The references in Capital are essentially the same,
with emphasis on socialist production, rational planning,
and human development. It could be argued that these are
theoretical statements on the necessity of planned economy (and they are that), but not theoretical statements
concerning praxis, nonetheless the praxis motif is there.
The two I have selected are as follows:

The life-process of society, which is based
on the process of material production, does not
strip off its mystical veil until it is treated
as production by freely associated men, and is
consciously regulated by them in accordance
with a settled plan [Capital I 80, my empha-
sis].

Freedom in this field [i.e., of production]
cannot consist of anything else but the fact
that socialized mankind, the associated pro-
ducers, regulate their interchange with Nature
rationally, bring it under their common control, instead of being ruled by it as by some
blind power, and accomplish their task with the
least expenditure of energy and under such
conditions as are proper and worthy for human
beings. Nevertheless, this always remains a
realm of necessity. Beyond it begins that
development of human potentiality for its own
sake, the true realm of freedom,[146] which however can only flourish upon that realm of
necessity as its basis.[147]

The experience of human consciousness is emergent
from material-social existence and actualized through
human activity; activity which is effectively human in

direct relation to the degree that it is planned and organized, in advance, in ways and structures which are compatible with the existing forces of production, the social nature of reality and the species-nature of humans.

> Of course, the consciousness of men will continue to be determined by the material processes that reproduce their society, even when men have come to regulate their social relations in such a way that these contribute best to the free development of all. But when these material processes have been made rational and have become the conscious work of men, the blind dependence of consciousness on social conditions will cease to exist. Reason, when determined by rational social conditions, is determined by itself. Socialist freedom embraces both sides of the relation between consciousness and social existence. The principle of historical materialism leads to its self-negation.[148]

C. Summary

Marx, from the perspective of political, social and economic analysis, provides a discussion and analysis of the nature of the ongoing process of human history, and by application, we gain the following notions which have pertinence for understanding the relationship of consciousness to the human capacity to intervene in history:

(i) The social character of reality.

(ii) The natural, social, historical and species-nature (in both aspects, i.e., species-relationship between individuals, and self-consciousness), of human individuals in society.

(iii) The locus of value, and the goal of human history is the development of the species-individuals' powers and capacities. This goal is historical. It is not an external norm.

(iv) Conscious information and knowledge of our contemporary and historical world is possible through conceptualization of, and empirically testing sense perception, as demonstrated in natural science and the development of industry.

(v)   Knowledge of the world and society is also revised and corrected by <u>theoretical</u> and <u>practical</u> criticism of existing theories and actual situations.

(vi)   Conscious persons have the capacity subjectively to transcend their existence, to theorize, and to develop new ideas. These ideas however find their force only in giving direction or incentive to human practical activity which can change the material and structural conditions in which species-individuals are productive and reproductive.

(vii) Human activity to be effectively <u>human</u>, must be socially organized and rationally planned, i.e., for the future, in response to knowledge of the nature of reality, and past activity and experience.

(viii) When making planning decisions for the future of society, species-individuals must deal with questions of the compatibility between certain types of material, structural and cultural conditions, and the development of human powers and capacities.

Chapter II - Notes

1. A detailed summary, of the issues with which this study is concerned and the representative perspectives in Marxist theory which this study utilizes, is in the Introduction of the study.

2. Karl Marx, A Contribution to the Critique of Political Economy, edited by Maurice Dobb (New York: International Publishers; New World Paperbacks, 1970), pp. 20f, hereafter referred to as Critique.

   In its "determinist" form this principle is well represented by Marvin Harris, in The Rise of Anthropological Theory (New York: Thomas Y. Crowell Company, 1968), p. 4:

   > "This principle [techno-environmental and techno-economic determinism] holds that similar technologies applied to similar environments tend to produce similar arrangements of labor in production and distribution, and that these in turn call forth similar kinds of social groupings, which justify and coordinate their activities by means of similar systems of values and beliefs. Translated into research strategy, the principle of techno-environmental, techno-economic determinism assigns priority to the study of the material conditions of sociocultural life, much as the principle of natural selection assigns priority to the study of differential reproductive success.
   >
   > The strategy in question will at once strike the sensitized reader as a form of materialism, and, indeed, I shall refer to it throughout this book as the strategy of 'cultural materialism'

   This perspective is also developed by Althusser, in For Marx, see especially pp. 107-111.

3. Karl Korsch, in Karl Marx (New York: Russell & Russell, 1963), pp. 185-88, provides an excellent short discussion of the dynamic and practical aspects of Marx's theory.

   For a discussion of why Marx is "misinterpreted in a mechanistic manner" see Jurgen Habermas, Theory and Practice (Boston: Beacon Press, 1973), pp. 168ff.

4. Karl Marx, Economic and Philosophical Manuscripts in Karl Marx: Early Writings, translated and edited by T.B. Bottomore (New York: McGraw-Hill, 1964), pp. 206-09, hereafter referred to as EPM.

   Bertell Ollman, in Alienation: Marx's Conception of Man in a Capitalist Society (Cambridge: Cambridge University Press, 1971) makes a compelling, if somewhat overstated, case for the proposition that Marx is a "relational" thinker in the tradition of Spinoza, Leibniz and Hegel (51). He argues that to understand Marx we must conceive society "relationally," i.e., that we must understand the relations as "internal" to each social factor.

5. For an excellent brief supportive discussion of the understanding of dialectical materialism in the biological and physical
sciences, see Needham, _Order and Life_, pp. 44-48.

Howard Selsam, David Boldway & Harry Martel, in _Dynamics of
Social Change: A Reader in Marxist Social Science_, New World
Paperbacks (New York: International Publishers, 1970), p. 26,
write:

> "Applied to history, materialism means only that before men can
> have governments, religions or philosophies, they must have
> food, shelter and, on much of the earth, clothing--in other
> words, the _material_ prerequisites of life.
>
> "By _historical_ Marx and Engels mean that human existence can
> be understood only as a _process_ _of_ _social_ _development_. Every-
> thing in our lives--our way of making a living, our tools and
> skills, the houses we live in and the clothes we wear, our
> social and political institutions, our knowledge, our ideas,
> our beliefs--all are part of a continuous pattern of social
> movement and social change. Thus there can be no adequate
> explanation of any question facing man unless that question is
> viewed _historically_."

For another excellent (and similar) discussion of Marx's
understanding of "materialism," see John Lewis, _The Marxism of Marx_
(London: Lawrence & Wishart, 1972), pp. 76ff.

6. Karl Marx and Frederick Engels, _The German Ideology_, edited by
C.J. Arthur, (New York: International Publishers, New World
Paperbacks, 1970), pp. 48-52, hereafter referred to as GI.

7. See especially Appendices, 1, 2, & 3, which are excerpts from
letters written by Engels in 1890, 1893, and 1894 on this issue.

Harris, in _Rise of Anthropological Theory_, pp. 242-45, also
makes use of this Engels correspondence to demonstrate that materialism is not a single factor theory of causation.

Mao makes the same point, without reference to Engels, in Stuart
R. Schram, _The Political Thought of Mao Tse-tung_, revised and
enlarged edition (New York: Praeger Publishers, 1972), pp. 199-200:

> ". . . we recognize that in the development of history as a whole
> it is material things that determine spiritual things and social
> existence that determines social consciousness, we also do and
> must recognize the reaction of spiritual things and social
> consciousness upon social existence and the reaction of the
> superstructure upon the economic foundation. This . . . is the
> avoidance of mechanistic materialism and the firm upholding of
> dialectical materialism . . ."

8. Frederick Engels, _Anti-Duhring_ (New York: International Publishers, 1939; New World Paperbacks, 1972), pp. 15-19.

9. In this sense nature as well as society is understood as social; as Korsch points out in Karl Marx, pp. 189-97, Marxist Materialism replaces "pure nature" with nature "mediated and modified through social activity and thus at the same time capable of a further change and modification by our own present and future activity, . . . [191]" He continues:

    "Being 'social,' nature has a specifically historical character varying in the different epochs. . . . For example, as emphasized by Marx in his controversy with Feuerbach, that cherry tree before the philosopher's window, whose ancestors were 'artifically' transplanted to Europe a few hundred years ago, is thereby for the modern European no nature-given growth; . . . [191]"

The social nature of humans is discussed by Lewis, Marxism of Marx, pp. 69 & 121, and by Ollman, in Alienation, pp. 106ff.

10. The social nature of reality as used here and by Marx is a cnceptualization which is a statement about the internal and external structures and mutual relations of all factors in reality (see Chapter I). Its parallel category is "internal relations" in Ollman, and it includes the category of causation as discussed by Whitehead in his explanation of the ontological principle (see Chapter I). For an excellent, more classical, discussion of causation which is also generally consonant with Marxian and Whiteheadian understandings, see R.M. MacIver, Social Causation (Boston: Ginn and Co., 1942), pp. 5-69 & 269-90.

11. This same theoretical position is held by Engels in Anti-Duhring; see especially pp. 27-33.

12. Engels in Anti-Durhing, pp. 42f, writes:
    ". . . they [thought and consciousness] are products of the human brain and . . . man himself is a product of Nature, which has been developed in and along with its environment; whence it is self-evident that the products of the human brain, being in the last analysis also products of Nature, do not contradict the rest of nature but are in correspondence with it." See also pp. 15-19.

13. Habermas, Theory and Practice, p. 201.

14. Karl Marx, Grundrisse: Foundations of the Critique of Political Economy, translated with a Foreword by Martin Nicolaus (Middlesex, England: Penguin Books, 1973), pp. 156-57, hereafter referred to as Grundrisse.

15. See especially Grundrisse 156-65.

16. Cf. Habermas, Theory and Practice, pp. 26ff.

17. Ollman, Alienation, p. 204.

18. Karl Marx, *Capital*, Translated from the third German edition by Samuel Moore and Edward Aveling, Edited by Frederick Engels (New York: International Publishers, 1967), Vol. I, p. 310, hereafter referred to as *Capital*.

19. Antonio Gramsci holds a position consonant with this; see for example his discussion of ideology in *Selections From the Prison Notebooks* (New York: International Publishers, 1971), pp. 376-77. See also p. 321 of the same work for its editors' note on Gramsci's affirmation of ideas as a material force; a concept which Gramsci attributed to Marx.

20. Karl Marx, *The Poverty of Philosophy*, (New York: International Publishers, New World Paperbacks, 1963), p. 189, hereafter referred to as PP.

21. Karl Marx, *The 18th Brumaire of Louis Bonaparte* (New York: International Publishers, New World Paperbacks, 1963), p. 15, hereafter referred to as *18th Brumaire*.

22. Karl Marx, *Contribution to the Critique of Hegel's Philosophy of Right: Introduction*, in *Karl Marx: Early Writings*, translated and edited by T.B. Bottomore (New York: McGraw-Hill, 1964), p. 52, hereafter referred to as CHR. Marx, in this passage writes: "[i]t is clear that the arm of criticism cannot replace the criticism of arms. Material force can only be overthrown by material force; but theory itself becomes a material force when it has seized the masses."

23. "'The ideas which the French Revolution gave rise to did not, however, lead beyond the *system* that it wanted to abolish by force.'
    Ideas can never lead beyond an old world system but only beyond the ideas of the old world system. Ideas cannot carry anything out at all. In order to carry out ideas men are needed who dispose of a certain practical force." (Karl Marx, *The Holy Family* [Moscow: Foreign Languages Publishing House, 1956], p. 160, hereafter referred to as HF.)

24. Recall Whitehead's discussion of "negative judgment," and see Marx's discussion of Proudhon in HF 59-64.

25. For an elaboration of the role ideas in Whitehead see above pp. 23ff, and in Marx see below pp. 77ff.

26. Bottomore footnotes Marx's use of the category in *On the Jewish Question*, in *Karl Marx: Early Writings*, p. 13:
        "The terms 'species-life' (*Gattungsleben*) and 'species-being' (Gattungswesen) are derived from Feuerbach. . . . Feuerbach discusses the nature of man, and argues that man is to

122

be distinguished from animals not by 'consciousness' as such, but by a particular kind of consciousness. Man is not only conscious of himself as an individual; he is also conscious of himself as a member of the human species, and so he apprehends a 'human essence' which is the same in himself and in other men. According to Feuerbach this ability to conceive of 'species' is the fundamental element in the human power of reasoning: 'Science is the consciousness of species.' Marx, while not departing from this meaning of the terms, employs them in other contexts; and he insists more strongly than Feuerbach that since this 'species-consciousness' defines the nature of man, man is only living and acting authentically (i.e. in accordance with his nature) when he lives and acts deliberately as a 'species-being,' that is, as a social being."

27. Karl Marx, On the Jewish Question, in Karl Marx: Early Writings, translated and edited by T.B. Bottomore (New York: McGraw-Hill, 1964), pp. 25, 26 & 30, hereafter referred to as JQ.
    It is worth emphasizing again that "human nature" as a concept, for Marx, is not a "static," Platonic, or Aristotelian "nature"; it is historical, relational and emergent. As Gramsci writes in Prison Notesbooks, p. 355, "human nature" is the "complex of social relations" and "it includes the idea of becoming (man 'becomes', he changes continuously with the changing of social relations) . . ." See also Appendix 4, of this study, for a more extended reference to Gramsci's "Marxist" understanding of the nature of humans. And yet another similar discussion can be found in Lewis, The Marxism of Marx, especially, pp. 22, 55f, 69, & 102f.

28. See also HF 156f and JQ 15-31.

29. For the earlier (i.e., 1844), more philosophical, but almost identical statement of how human production is manifestation and realization of our human and species-character, see the quotation from "Excerpt Notes of 1844," in Appendix number 5.

30. See also HF 175-76.

31. "In his only organized treatment of the subject, Marx presents alienation as partaking of four broad relations which are so distributed as to cover the whole of human existence. These are man's relations to his productive activity, his product, other men, and the species.*" Ollman, Alienation, p. 137. See also pp. 131-36.
    Lewis, in The Marxism of Marx, p. 114, notes that for Marx the full development of human individuals is the overcoming of alienation.
    See also Herbert Marcuse, Reason and Revolution (New York: Humanities Press, 1954), pp. 273ff.

*This quotation contains a footnote which reads: "The account referred to appears in the 1844 Manuscripts, pp. 69-80."

32. We have noted the category of species-ness in Marx's early writings and in the Grundrisse. It also emerges in Capital: "When the labourer co-operates systematically with others, he strips off the fetters of his individuality, and develops the capabilities of his species [Capital I 329]."

33. To discuss the nature of history or society, in a Marxist sense, is not to discuss a metaphysical position, but rather to discuss history and society descriptively and historically. In my judgment Korsch in Karl Marx, p. 168 is correct when he writes:
"Even where Marx departs from that purely critical position, he does not lay down any general propositions as to the essential nature of all society but merely describes the particular conditions and developmental tendencies inherent in the his- torical form of contemporary bourgeois society."
Another "Marxist," George Lukacs, in History and Class Con- sciousness (Cambridge, Massachusetts: MIT Press, 1971), frequently implies an ahistorical ontology (e.g., the use of the category "essence of man," p. xxiv), but he writes affirmatively of the Marxist perspective in which "the meaning of history is to be found in the process of history itself and not, as formerly, in a transcendental, mythological or ethical meaning foisted on to recalcitrant material, . . . [p. 22]"

34. It must be emphasized that "eternal object" is a Whiteheadian term, and that for Marx, there are no "eternal" objects or forms.

35. For three more important passages from the Grundrisse which illustrate Marx's process view of the production process, see Appendices 6, 7 and 8.
The necessary and coherent relationship of Marx's economic categories is implicit also in Capital. This is developed by Pixley, in "Whitehead y Marx sobre la Dinamica de la Historia," in Louis Althusser y Etienne Balibar, Para Leer el Capital (Mexico: Siglo XXI Editores, 1969), where he writes, p. 87:
"Marx's fundamental concepts are presented in chapter 4, 5, 6, and 10 of the first Volume of Capital. . . . What is of interest to us is that even the concepts that seem to be taken from the ordinary langue, such as value, work, and capital [in addition to exchange value, use value and price] acquire a new meaning and a new precision when presented in their systematic relation. The communist philosopher Louis Althusser understands that this structuralist logic is the discovery of major philosophical interest in the work of Marx." [my translation].

36. The position summarized in this paragraph is developed by Ollman in _Alienation_, with the exception that in his effort to emphasize internal relations, he fails to develop external relations. We will deal with this problem further in Chapter III.

37. Gramsci, in _Prison Notebooks_, p. 351, writes of people as a process of their own activities.

38. Habermas, _Theory and Practice_, p. 248.

39. V.I. Lenin, _Materialism and Empirio-Criticism_ (New York: International Publishers, 1927), p. 34. Also cf. Karl Korsch, _Marxism and Philosophy_, p. 73.

40. For an excellent discussion of Marx's "inversion of Hegel" see Louis Althusser, _For Marx_ (New York: Random House, Vintage, 1970), pp. 87-116 & 173ff. He makes a compelling case for his claim that "_Marx_ _did_ _not_ _retain_ _the_ _terms_ _of_ _the_ _Hegelian_ _model_ _of_ _society_ _and_ '_invert_' _them_. He substituted other, only distantly related terms for them. Furthermore, he overhauled the _connexion_ which had previously ruled over the terms. For Marx, _both_ _terms_ and _relation_ changed in nature and sense [109]."
  Marcuse, in _Reason and Revolution_, p. 258, takes a very similar position; for example he writes:
      ". . . all the philosophical concepts of Marxian theory are social and economic categories, whereas Hegel's social and economic categories are all philosophical concepts. . . . Every single concept in the Marxian theory has a materially different foundation. . . .
  As a first approach to the problem, we may say that in Hegel's system all categories terminate in the existing order, while in Marx's they refer to the negation of this order." (See also 313ff.)

41. Engels, _Anti-Duhring_, p. 30.

42. _Ibid._

43. _Ibid._ Because ideas, for Marxist theory, are historical and not eternal does not make them unreal. For an excellent passage on this point, see Engels, _Anti-Duhring_, p. 44.

44. Lenin, _Materialism and Empirio-Criticism_, pp. 63-64.

45. Schram, _Political Thought of Mao Tse-tung_, p. 187.

46. "Monsieur Proudhon has very well grasped the fact that men produce cloth, linen, silks, . . . What he has not grasped is that these men, according to their abilities, also produce the social relations amid which they prepare cloth and linen. Still less has he understood that men, who produce their social

relations in accordance with their material productivity, also produce _ideas_, _categories_, that is to say the abstract ideal expression of these same social relations. Thus the categories are no more eternal than the relations they express. They are historical and transitory products [PP 189]."

Engels develops this point theoretically in <u>Anti-Duhring</u>; see for example, pp. 44-46.

47. I have already discussed at length in this chapter another historical category which is primary to Marx, i.e., species-being.

48. "The 'fetish-character' of the commodity, reduced to its simplest form, consists in the fact that man's handiwork assumes a peculiar quality which influences in a fundamental way the actual behavior of the persons concerned. It does not wield that remarkable power (as the earlier economists had believed) by an eternal law of nature, yet it is endowed with such power under the particular social conditions prevailing in the present epoch of society." (Korsch, <u>Karl Marx</u>, p. 131).

"In other words, the materials that should serve life come to rule over its content and goal, and the consciousness of man is completely made victim to the relationships of material production." (Marcuse, <u>Reason and Revolution</u>, p. 273).

49. Lukacs, "Reification and the Consciousness of the Proletariat," in <u>History and Class Consciousness</u>, pp. 83-222. He writes for example, p. 135:
". . . man in capitalist society confronts a reality 'made' by himself (as a class) which appears to him to be a natural phenomenon alien to himself; he is wholly at the mercy of its 'laws', his activity is confined to the exploitation of the inexorable fulfillment of certain individual laws for his own (egoistic) interests. But even while 'acting' he remains, in the nature of the case, the object and not the subject of events."

50. "The statement that <u>labour time</u>, or the amount of labour, is the measure of values means nothing other than that the measure of labour is the measure of values. Two things are only commensurable if they are of the <u>same nature</u>. Products can be measured with the measure of labour--labour time--only because they are, by their nature, <u>labour</u>. They are objectified labour [<u>Grundrisse</u> 613]."

51. This is the subject of the category "use-value"; "Use value is not concerned with human activity as the source of the product, with its having been posited by human activity, but with its being for mankind [<u>Grundrisse</u> 613]."

52. Marcuse, Reason and Revolution, p. 280. See also p. 279.

53. Marx, Grundrisse 202, 223, 295, 298f.

54. Marx makes the comment in the Preface to Capital that even within the ruling-classes "a foreboding is dawning, that the present society is no solid crystal, but an organism capable of change, and is constantly changing [Capital I 10]."
    Korsch also makes this point in his discussion of "Marx's materialist criticism of the Hegelian idealist dialectic." He writes:
    "Marx's study of society is based upon a full recognition of the reality of historical change. Marx treats all conditions of existing bourgeois society as changing or, more exactly, as conditions being changed by human actions. At the same time, he regards all, even the most general categories of social science, as categories changeable and to be changed." (Korsch, Karl Marx, p. 55).

55. Jurgen Habermas, in Knowledge and Human Interests (Boston: Beacon Press, 1971), p. 260, makes this point when he writes:
    "But in our own self-formative process, we are at once both actor and critic. In the final instance, the meaning of the process itself must be capable of becoming part of our consciousness in a critical manner, entangled as we are in the drama of life history. . . . For the final state of a self-formative process is attained only if the subject remembers its identifications and alienations, the objectivations forced upon it and the reflections it arrived at, as the path upon which it constituted itself."

56. See the quotation (below p. 95) from Mao, in which he discusses conceptualization as the second stage of knowledge, Schram, Political Thought of Mao Tse-tung, p. 191.

57. See Chapter I for a discussion of negative judgments.

58. The emergence of Marxism as an analysis and criticism of capitalist society was itself a judgment and a proposition which became a real force in history. Korsch, Karl Marx, pp. 75-76.

59. For a discussion of alienated labor, see especially EPM, pp. 120-34.

60. See especially Capital I, pp. 235-302, 331, 360-64; and Vol. III, pp. 87-100.

61. Martin Nicolaus in his foreword to the Grundrisse writes:
". . . Marx's theoretical labours were not concerned with
economics for the sake of economics, philosophy for the sake of
philosophy, or criticism for its own sake; but rather that the
aim of this work was to prepare, to educate the next generation
of leaders of the working class in the objective preconditions,
possibility and necessity of the historic task [Grundrisse
24]."

62. Cf. Lewis, The Marxism of Marx, pp. 66-69.

63. Lenin, "What the 'Friends of the People' Are" (1894), Selected
Works, Vol. XI, p. 439, from Selsam, et al., Dynamics of Social
Change, pp. 81-82.
     Pixley also makes this point in "Whitehead y Marx Sobre la
Dinamica de la Historia," pp. 96-97:
     "Marx's materialism is by no means a mechanism. . . . Although
in his analysis of history he emphasizes as predominant the
efficient causality, he admits as well the final causality.
Violence, as Marx describes it, is a violence exercised by human
groups that pursue definite purposes. This type of activity is
directed towards purposes that are not realized yet, but are
only visualized in the heads of groups of men . . . [my
translation]"

64. Cf. Lewis, The Marxism of Marx, pp. 54, 69 & 72.

65. Engels, Anti-Duhring, p. 125.

66. Lenin, Materialism and Empirio-Criticism, p. 69. For further
discussion of the relationship of consciousness to existence, in the
same work, see especially pp. 38, 44, 48 & 83.

67. Korsch, Marxism and Philosophy, p. 77.

68. Ibid, p. 78.

69. Ibid, see also p. 80f.

70. Habermas, in Knowledge and Human Interest, p. 47f, makes
reference to this aspect of Marx's theory:
     "In the preliminary studies for the Critique of Political
Economy there is a model according to which the history of the
species is linked to an automatic transposition of natural
science and technology into a self-consciousness of the social
subject (general intellect)--a consciousness that controls the
material life process."
     See also p. 76, where he writes: "Science makes possible
technical control over processes of both nature and society."

71. See especially Marx, The Holy Family, pp. 124-25.

72. An Observer, "The Hungarian New Left: Sociology and Revolution," The Monthly Review 26 (April 1975), p. 37. I do not mean to imply that this notion either originates with or is unique to the "School of Budapest."

73. Ibid., pp. 37-38.

74. Gramsci, Prison Notebooks, p. 352.

75. For a further Marxist discussion of the capacity and limits of human conscious knowledge see Engels, Anti-Duhring, pp. 96-100.

76. This is the importance of his references to natural science, and to capitalism developing the material conditions through industry which will enable a new more human society; see especially EMP 163f, Capital I 592 & 763 where Marx again speaks of the "conscious technical application of science."

77. See also Korsch, Karl Marx, p. 133, and Lewis, The Marxism of Marx, p. 71.

78. Habermas makes the point when he writes in Knowledge and Human Interests, p. 210:
"For the conditions under which the human species constitutes itself are not just those posited by reflection. . . . the self-formative process is not unconditioned. It depends on the contingent conditions of both subjective and objective nature: conditions of the individuating socialization of interacting individuals on the one hand, and, on the other, those of the "material exchange" of communicatively acting persons with an environment that is to be made technically controllable."

79. Habermas, however, in Knowledge and Human Interests, pp. 52-56 and especially 281-87, argues that Marx developed a theory which combined both "self-generation through productive activity" and "self-formation through critical-revolutionary activity"; and while able to account for productive knowledge, he was unable to account for reflective knowledge. I will discuss this issue at greater length in the seccnd half of this chapter when I discuss the human capacity to theorize and to make reflective judgments.

80. "Change becomes a matter of man transforming his existence. From being a passive observer of development, as in Hegel, the individual has become the actor whose daily life brings it about." Ollman, Alienation, p. 36.

81. Ollman, in _Alienation_, pp. 116-20, discusses Marx's concern to link "freedom with full development of man's powers," and his (Marx's) position that only in community is "personal freedom possible" (118).

82. Martin Nicolaus, in the foreword of his translation of the _Grundrisse_, writes:

> "It becomes clear now that the real history of the world is not the product of a _sui generis_ 'Mind', but rather that this 'Mind' and all its relations are a product of the human head; and, moreover, of a human head anchored in real history, both driven and limited by particular, changing social-economic modes of existence; finally, a human head integrated into a sensual, material and social body which, by its conduct, can and does alter its history, and therefore alters also the sources and conditions of thought [_Grundrisse_ 33]."

83. See also Lenin, _Materialism and Empirio-Criticism_, especially pp. 38, 44, 48, 69 & 83.

84. Korsch, in _Karl Marx_, p. 83, presents a good expression of the effect of Marxist materialism on the quest for theoretical truth:

> "Materialistic criticism, which defines all theoretical truths as mere historical "forms of social consciousness," does in no way abandon the quest for theoretical truth, but only replaces the traditional concept of an absolute truth by a less ambitious and much more practical idea. Every truth, according to the Marxists, applies only to a definite set of conditions; it is therefore not absolute but relative, not independent and complete in itself, but contingent upon external facts. To-day's truth, then, depends upon the existing mode of material production and the class struggle arising therefrom. But this new definition of truth in no way lessens, nay, it enhances, the strictness of the formal demands which must be fulfilled by a 'true' proposition from the standpoint of materialistic science."

85. See also references to verification through praxis later in this chapter.

86. See Appendices 1, 2, and 3, and for a statement of the importance of the cultural aspect, see Gramsci, _Prison Notebooks_, p. 349. Cf. also Habermas, _Knowledge and Human Interests_, p. 42.

87. Althusser, in the context of a discussion on the materialist dialectic, which also draws on Mao's "On Contradiction," makes this similar statement in _For Marx_, pp. 212-13:

> ". . . Marxist theory and practice do not only approach unevenness in the form of simple exteriority (the _reciprocal action_ of infrastructure and superstructure), but in a form

organically _internal_ to each instance of the social totality, to each contradiction. It is 'economism' (mechanism) and not the true Marxist tradition that sets up the hierarchy of instances once and for all, . . . It is economism that identifies eternally in advance of the determinant-contradiction-in-the-last-instance with the _role_ of the dominant contradiction, which for ever assimilates such and such an 'aspect' (forces of production, economy, practice) to the principle _role_, and such and such another 'aspect' (relations of production, politics, ideology, theory) to the secondary _role_--whereas in real history determination in the last instance by the economy is exercised precisely in the permutations of the principal role between the economy, politics, theory, etc."
See also Korsch, _Marxism and Philosophy_, p. 60. And for a Marxist discussion of the reciprocity which exists in society between material conditions, social structures, technology, ideas, etc., see Lewis, _The Marxism of Marx_, pp. 71-75.

88. See also GI 107.

89. Schram, _Political Thought of Mao Tse-tung_, p. 191.

90. Mao writes from the same perspective in his discussion on theory and practice. Theory applied in practice is also tested theory. Mao writes:
    "But when Marxism emphasizes theory, it does so precisely and only because it can guide our actions. . . . The active effect of cognition manifests itself not only in the active leap from perceptual knowledge to rational knowledge, but also, and more importantly, in the leap from rational knowledge to revolutionary practice. . . . The problem whether theories correspond to objective realities is not entirely solved in the process of cognition from the perceptual to the rational as mentioned before; there it cannot be entirely solved. The only way to solve this problem completely is to redirect rational knowledge to social practice and apply theory to practice to see whether it can achieve preconceived results. . . ." (Schram, _Political Thought of Mao Tse-tung_, p. 193).

91. "_Ad hominem_" (lit., to the man) here probably means an argument directed at or "appealing to a prejudice, emotion, or a special interest rather than to intellect or reason." (_Random House College Dictionary_).

92. While Marx does not develop the concept of "interests," Habermas, in _Knowledge and Human Interests_, p. 196, does so in a way which adds depth to Marx's use of the term, and in a way which is consonant with the rest of Marx's theory. Habermas writes:
    "Knowledge-constitutive interests mediate the natural history of the human species with the logic of its self-formative pro-

cess. . . . I term _interests_ the basic orientations rooted in specific fundamental conditions of the possible reproduction and self-constitution of the human species, namely _work_ and _interaction_. Hence these basic orientations do not aim at the gratification of immediately empirical needs but at the solution of system problems in general." See also pp. 203 & 211ff.

93. Korsch, _Karl Marx_, p. 174.

94. Cf. Lewis, _The Marxism of Marx_, pp. 51 & 54.

95. Lenin, _Materialism and Empirio-Criticism_, p. 337.

96. Marx writes in the preface of the "Third Manuscript": "It is hardly necessary to assure the reader who is familiar with political economy that my conclusions are the fruit of an entirely empirical analysis, based upon a careful critical study of political economy [EPM 63]." This statement gains credibility when one surveys the data on working conditions; see for example _Capital_ I pp. 231-302 and _Capital_ III pp. 87ff.

97. As Lewis comments in _The Marxism of Marx_, p. 21: "knowledge for Marx was the process of going to meet reality, getting to grips with it, and verifying it in the light of experience, and trying again."

98. Korsch, _Marxism and Philosophy_, p. 71.

99. For a detailed Marxist discussion on the importance of doing theory, read Althusser, _For Marx_, pp. 9-39, 167-73, and especially p. 167, where he writes:
   "By theory, in this respect [what theory _itself_, and its relation to 'social practice' are for Marxism], I shall mean a specific _form_ _of_ _practice_, itself belonging to the complex unity of the 'social practice' of a determinate human society. Theoretical practice falls within the general definition of practice. It works on a raw material (representations, concepts, facts) which it is given by other practices, whether 'empirical', 'technical' or 'ideological'."

100. Ollman, _Alienation_, p. 51. This quotation and its position-- that the _ought_ is ascertained in the _is_--will be discussed in detail in the following pages. This is an important concept because it is the method by which the concept "human development" gets its meaning and content.

101. Gramsci, _Prison Notebooks_, pp. 370-71.

102. Althusser, _For Marx_, pp. 219-47.
   For an excellent Marxist influenced, but _liberal-democratic_, development, see C.B. Macpherson, _Democratic Theory: Essays in_

Retrieval (Oxford, Clarendon Press, 1973), pp. 3-76, and for an excerpt, see Appendix 9.

103. Althusser, For Marx, pp. 242-47.

104. Althusser, For Marx, p. 247.

105. Engels, Anti-Duhring, pp. 94-130.

106. Ibid., p. 105.

107. Ibid.

108. Cf. Gramsci, "Moral Science and Historical Materialism," in Prison Notebooks, pp. 409-10.

109. Gramsci, Prison Notebooks, p. 133, my emphasis. See also my discussion (above p. 90) of the human capacity to consciously transcend and understand empirical existence.

110. "Truth, in short, is not a realm apart from historical reality, nor a region of eternally valid ideas. To be sure, it transcends the given historical reality, but only in so far as it crosses from one historical stage to another." Marcuse, Reason and Revolution, p. 315.

111. Ollman, Alienation, p. 76.

112. Ibid.

113. Ibid., pp. 75-86.

114. "A commodity is a use-value because it has the power to satisfy some human need." Ollman, Alienation, p. 184.

115. In this context we can understand Korsch's comment in Karl Marx, p. 128:
". . . Capital is only nominally the subject of Marx's new economic theory. Its real theme is labour both in its present-day economic form of subjugation by capital and in its development, through the revolutionary struggle of the proletariat, to a new directly social and socialist condition."

116. Karl Marx, Critique of the Gotha Programme, Little Marx Library (New York: International Publishers, 1966), hereafter referred to as CGP.

117. "Marx's idea of a rational society implies an order in which it is not the universality of labor but the universal satisfaction of all individual potentialities that constitutes the princi-

133

ple of social organization." (Marcuse, Reason and Revolution, p. 293).

"And does the concept of science as 'creation' not then mean that it too is 'politics'? Everything depends on seeing whether the creation involved is 'arbitrary', or whether it is rational--i.e., 'useful' to men in that it enlarges their concept of life, and raises to a higher level (develops) life itself." (Gramsci, Prison Notebooks, p. 245).

118. "It is of the utmost importance to note that Marx views the abolition of private property entirely as a means of the abolition of alienated labor, and not as an end in itself." Marcuse, Reason and Revolution, p. 282.

119. Karl Marx and Friedrich Engels, "Manifesto of the Communist Party," in Marx and Engels: Basic Writings on Politics and Philosophy, edited by Lewis S. Feuer, Anchor Books (Garden City, New York: Doubleday, 1959), p. 29.

120. See pp. 83ff, 90, 92ff, 94f, 97-102, 108ff of this study for discussions of the various aspects of the method for establishing an empirically discerned normative reference for human society. The method is the ascertaining, through praxis, of the possible and the ought to be from the is. The method includes: the experience of the human capacity to consciously transcend and understand empirical existence, and to act in response to that understanding. It includes the study of science, history, philosophy, economic, political and social theory, and critical reflection on empirical observations of actual productive, social and cultural conditions and activity in human society.

121. See EPM 165-67. Also Korsch, in Karl Marx, argues against the notions that Marxism is "utopian" and that it attempts to portray future society. His position is balanced when he writes:
    "On the other hand, Marxism, while carefully avoiding a detailed painting of the future stages, nevertheless endeavors to find, within contemporary bourgeois society, the main tendencies of a further development leading up, first to that transitional stage opened by the proletarian revolution, and ultimately, to those further advanced stages which Marx called a completely developed communistic society [p. 53]."

122. Korsch, Karl Marx, pp. 204-05. This quotation also contains a footnote which reads: "See Marx, Marginal Notes to the Programme of the German Labour Party, 1875 (Neue Zeit, IX, i, 1891, pp. 563-75) and the concluding sentence of the second section of the Communist Manifesto, . . ."

123. ". . . restoration of the category of use-value to the center of economic analysis means a sharp questioning of the economic

process as to whether and how it fills the real needs of individuals." Marcuse, Reason and Revolution, pp. 303f.

124. Mao is more explicit than Marx in delineating the three aspects (material forces, socio-economic structures and culture), and their reciprocal influence. He writes:
"True, the productive forces, practice, and the economic foundation generally manifest themselves as the principal and decisive factors; whoever denies this is not a materialist. But under certain conditions, such aspects as the relations of production, theory, and the superstructure in turn manifest themselves as the principal and decisive factors; this must also be admitted." (Schram, Political Thought of Mao Tse-tung, p. 199. See also above pp. 45f.)

125. At least in his early years Marx did not assume that communism was the final human social form, in EPM, p. 167, he wrote: "Communism is the necessary form and the dynamic principle of the immediate future, but communism is not itself the goal of human development--the form of human society." For the longer passage from which this is drawn, see Appendix 10.

126. For supporting evidence of Marx's broad base of study, see Lewis, The Marxism of Marx, pp. 33-35.

127. Korsch, Karl Marx, p. 179. See also p. 189.

128. "The development of fixed capital indicates to what degree general social knowledge has become a direct force of production, and to what degree, hence, the conditions of the process of social life itself have come under the control of the general intellect and been transformed in accordance with it. To what degree the powers of social production have been produced, not only in the form of knowledge, but also as immediate organs of social practice, of the real life process [Grundrisse 706]." (See also Capital I, p. 763.)

129. "Free time - which is both idle time and time for higher activity - has naturally transformed its possessor into a different subject, and he then enters into the direct production process as this different subject. This process is then both discipline, as regards the human being in the process of becoming; and, at the same time, practice [Ausubung], experimental science, materially creative and objectifying science, as regards the human being who has become, in whose head exists the accumulated knowledge of society [Grundrisse 712]."

130. Schram, Political Thought of Mao Tse-tung, p. 194. For a more complete discussion see pp. 190-201.

131. "Marx had understood and described the proletariat's struggle for freedom in terms of the dialectical unity of theory and practice." Lukacs, _History and Class Consciousness_, p. 41.

132. "The dialectical interpretation comprehends the knowing subject in terms of the relations of social praxis, in terms of its position, both within the process of social labor and the process of enlightening the political forces about their goals." Habermas, _Theory and Practice_, pp. 210-11. See pp. 253ff.

133. Althusser, in _For Marx_, p. 229, writes: "He [Marx] replaced the old postulates (empiricism/idealism of the subject, empiricism/idealism of the essence) which were the basis not only for idealism but also for pre-Marxist materialism, by a historico-dialectical materialism of praxis; . . ."

134. Gramsci, _Letters from Prison_, p. 240. See also pp. 240-242; and pp. xxi of the Introduction to _Prison Notebooks_ for references which imply that Gramsci understands that Marx uses the concept of praxis in the _Holy Family_.

135. See also the discussion of, and the references to, Lenin in the following pages of this study.

136. Korsch, _Marxism and Philosophy_, pp. 82-83.

137. Gramsci, _Prison Notebooks_, p. 365.

138. Karl Marx, _Theses on Feuerbach_ in _Karl Marx: Selected Writings in Sociology and Social Philosophy_, translated by T.B. Bottomore (New York: McGraw-Hill, 1956), p. 67, hereafter referred to as TF.

139. For a discussion of the Second Thesis in the context of the struggle against subjective idealism, and to affirm the reality of things-in-themselves, see Lenin, _Materialism and Empirio-Criticism_, pp. 100-03.

140. Schram, _Political Thought of Mao Tse-tung_, p. 183.
   See also Engel's discussion of modern, dialectical materialism in _Anti-Duhring_, especially pp. 30, 31, 152 & 292.
   Korsch, in _Karl Marx_, pp. 175f, also elaborates on Marx's divergence from Feuerbach.

141. Lenin, _Materialism and Empirio-Criticism_, p. 136. See also pp. 33, 34, 63, & 64.

142. _Ibid._, p. 106. For further references to practice as the verification of thought and theory, see pp. 99, 100, 136, 139, 142 & 192.

143. As I noted earlier in this section, the development of "praxis" as a theory of verification and of "revolutionary practice," was done by later Marxists. This does not mean that the elements of praxis theory are not in Marx's writings, nor that developed praxis theory is dissonant with Marx.

144. Cf. Lewis, The Marxism of Marx, pp. 51 & 54.

145. "As the practice of changing objective existing conditions based upon certain ideas, theories, plans, or programmes moves forward step by step, man's knowledge of objective reality also deepens step by step. The movement or change of the world of objective realities is never finished, hence man's recognition of truth through practice is also never complete. Marxism-Leninism has in no way put an end to the discovery of truths, but continually [putuan-ti] blazes the path toward the recognition of truths through practice. Our conclusion is that we stand for the concrete and historical unity of the subjective and the objective, of theory and practice, of knowledge and action, . . ." Schram, Poltical Thought of Mao Tse-tung, pp. 193-94.

146. The concluding sentence of Korsch's essay "The Problem of Marxism and Philosophy," in Marxism and Philosophy, p. 126 reads: "Socialism, both in its ends and in its means, is a struggle to realize freedom." (Emphasis in original).

147. Marx, Capital III, as translated by Bottomore, in Karl Marx: Selected Writings, pp. 254-55 (my emphasis).
Or as Lewis in The Marxism of Marx, p. 115, summarizes: "We then have the whole structure of Marxism as built around social labour (a) producing man himself and his world, (b) proceeding by exploitation and creating alienation, (c) transcending class society to release the forces of production, overcome alienation, and achieve fully social labour and fully developed man."

148. Marcuse, Reason and Revolution, pp. 319f.

CHAPTER III

POSSIBLE IMPLICATIONS OF WHITEHEAD'S
UNDERSTANDING FOR MARXIST THEORY

In this chapter I will refer to the material in the first two chapters and discuss six important problem areas in Marxist theory. I will not attempt a resolution of these questions but I will raise the questions and explore the possible ways these questions may be clarified, by-passed and/or answered when addressed with the assistance of the understanding and/or application of the process paradigm. All of these questions are fundamentally important aspects of the concern of this study, i.e., a theoretical discussion of the human capacity to intervene consciously in the historical process. The questions discussed will include the idealism-materialism problem, the freedom-determinism question, the epistemological question, the normative referent for guiding conscious intervention in the historical process, the timing of effective intervention, and the question of compatibility between desired experiences and social environment.

There are three general ways in which Whitehead's theoretical scheme, if understood in its wholeness, and applied to the Marxist theoretical scheme, could be helpful to the development of social theory in general and to Marxist theorists in particular, as they are concerned with the human capacity to intervene consciously in history. The first of these is a general statement and only will be mentioned here; a substantive discussion of the latter two, in terms of the six specific questions listed above, is the purpose of this chapter.

First, in light of the work of relational philosophers, e.g., Spinoza, Leibniz and Hegel, and modern biology[1] and physics, Whitehead's development, in Process and Reality, of a process-relational model, gives credibility to process-relational theory. In this context, the cogency of Whitehead's theoretical scheme enables one to understand Ollman's language and content in Alienation, and lends credence to the possibility that Marx was influenced by and struggling with relational concepts. Understanding Whitehead certainly influences the way one understands the Grundrisse (given the process-relational language in that important work), and increases the ease with which it is read and understood. The first statement, then, is simply an affirmation that, in general, Whitehead's theoretical scheme provides a world view within which Marxist theory becomes increasingly rational and cogent.

Second, Whitehead's process model provides the possibility of overcoming or putting in a new perspective three major dualisms, (i) idealism vs. materialism, (ii) freedom vs. determinism, and (iii) knower vs. known, or the epistemological problem. This possibility will be the subject of the first section of this chapter.

Third, as we will explore in the second section of this chapter, Whitehead's theoretical scheme may, if applied, have a contribution to Marxist theory not only for understanding reality but also in its capacity as a theory for changing reality.

A.   Possible Implications of a Paradigm Shift from a "Materialist" Model to a "Process" Model

It is difficult to know whether to speak of a "paradigm" shift or a "linguistic" shift, since, as Ollman has shown, there is convincing evidence that Marx was working out of an implicit relational model.   When I speak of a paradigm shift, I do not mean to imply that Marx was not a relational theorist (since, in general, I agree with Ollman on this point), but to look at the possible implications of a linguistic-conceptual shift, since Marx did for the most part use materialist language, which carries with it the historically accrued meanings of the language. Thus to the Marxist I say: understanding and using Whitehead's categories will assist you in making your case and keep you from either "crude materialism" or "ethical humanism." And to the non-Marxist I say: if you read and try to understand Marx in the context of an understanding of Whitehead's categories, he is more readable and increasingly coherent and cogent.

1.   Implications for the Idealist-Materialist Problem in Marxist Theory

The problem is that neither the category "material", nor "ideal" or "idea", is inclusive of human experience or reality as we have come to understand it.   Thus neither materialism nor idealism as a category or theory can be affirmed without qualification and/or supplementation by the other, and each can be rejected if it is posited as the central category of a world view or social paradigm. Marxist materialism (according to my interpretation and the interpretation of the range of Marxists used in this study) is not mechanistic, and Marxist theory does include a theoretical description of the role of ideas and subjective freedom. I attempted to demonstrate these points in the first half of Chapter II. The problem is rather that Marxist categories themselves may require a defensive explanation. That is to say, it is accepted by Marxist and non-Marxist alike that Marxist theory is "materialist"; this then requires not only explication for understanding, but it produces problems. Even though I do not argue that ideas or concepts exist without a material base, or doubt that a material base can exist without ideas; and though I agree that ideas and concepts are neither reducible to material factors nor are they a necessary sub-category of the category "material," the problems still exist. Why? Because "material," "form" or "idea," and "subjective will" are each abstractions from our experience of reality, and to use one of the categories as descriptive of the perspective or model is immediately to confuse the problems at hand. Harris, for example, claims that "Marx and Engels were the first to show how the problem of consciousness and subjective experience of the importance of ideas for behavior could be reconciled with causation on the physicalist model."[2] My point is that Marx, and Marxists like Harris, can affirm both the power of ideas and a principle of social causation, but cannot show theoretically within the "materialist" paradigm how the two are reconciled.

In German Ideology, Marx writes of the "First Premises of Materialist Method [GI 42]." As a method it means simply that any study of human history must begin with physical and organizational existence. And Marx's method, analysis and conclusions have demonstrated their contribution to socio-economic theory and change. Nonetheless, the category, which provides the overall focus of the method, focuses only on the beginning point and not inclusively upon all which must be studied if human society and history are to be understood and intentionally changed.

It may well be the case that Marx was writing against "idealism", and thus needed to balance an incorrect analysis of the origin and role of ideas in human history; nonetheless, if Marx is a relational theorist of human society (and I believe his analysis, if not his categories demonstrate this), then it may be helpful if we see how process or relational categories facilitate the understanding of Marx's writings, and the doing of a Marxist analysis, particularly with reference to the materialism-idealism question.

In the process model as developed by Whitehead the overall descriptive category is "process" and within that model the central category of analysis is the "actual occasion" or "actual event." As _materialism_ or _idealism_ is replaced by _process_, so the central place of _material_ or idea is replaced by _event_. The significance of this is that the category "actual event" _by definition_ includes the abstract factors (i) actual data, i.e., material, (ii) idea, i.e., form or structure, and (iii) subjectivity. And furthermore it is _by definition_ internally related to other events in its environment and in its past and future; at the same time it maintains uniqueness and individuality. In its _individual_ character it has the quality of being externally related to both its environment and to motion. A description of "actual event" as a primary category of analysis, and of each of its abstract factors, is developed in Chapter I; the point I want to make here is that the category of "actual event" is inclusive of the variables which are at odds in a materialist-idealist discussion, that is to say, "actual event" does not by definition produce the conflict which materialism does.

This is not to say that we are not still faced with the study, analysis and description of the role and force, etc., of each of the _abstract_ variables (i.e., material-structural data, ideas and subjectivity); it is however to say that we do not begin our theoretical efforts by saddling our _abstract_ categories with meanings, with which etymologically, they are overburdened. I emphasize the fact that these variables are _abstract_ to point out that as long as this emphasis is maintained, there is less danger of any of the variables gaining the suffix "ism" with the result that the rest of the variables will be defined in terms of _the one_.

In more specific terms: does this mean we have solved the materialist-idealist problem? And what does this mean for social theory? I will discuss the related epistemological question later; at this point I will discuss first the materialist-idealist question, understanding _idea_ as _form_, and then discuss idea as conscious conceptualization which in its complex form is proposition or theory.

The materialist-idealist problem is not solved, rather it becomes a non-problem when both material and idea (form), are viewed as abstract constructions of a complex whole. If we begin with the assumptions (i) that there is no _actual_ material without _actual_ idea (form), and vice versa, and (ii) that the conceptions _material_ and

142

form are abstract, heuristic, conscious mental constructs which help us to conceptualize, understand and intentionally control and change our environment and life experience, then the problem is not material vs. idea or form, but (i) the relationship of these abstract variables, (ii) when, and to what extent they gain enough real independence within the process, and (iii) when and to what extent they are accessible to intentional leverage for control and change. For example, to again use the example in Chapter I, if we want the children of Boston to have the experience of access to free medical care, the issue is not do we change the quantity and quality of material conditions involved or do we change the form (idea) of the health-care delivery system; nor do we assume that one is the function of the other and therefore to change the fundamental one is to change the other. Rather we must deal with each as one of the abstract interrelated variables of a complex whole, with the awareness that each may be in any moment the most important variable on which to focus attention and action for the desired control or change in our consciously directed efforts to gain the desired experience for the Boston children. The categories "process," "actual event," and their subcategories facilitate such theoretical analysis, as does Marxist theory, with the exception that a "materialist" method has a built-in bias as to what will be the significant variable. I will discuss this further below, but first I must discuss another way of posing the materialist-idealist question.

Frequently the issue is posed by social theorists as material-structural reality (i.e., means and relations of production) versus conscious conceptual, cultural, or ideological reality. That is to say, foundation vs. superstructure, or in a more subtle form structural-anthropology vs. cultural anthropology.[3] This issue was discussed in Chapters I and II in the sections on the origin and place of ideas. Process and Marxist theorists concur on several important points.[4] (i) They agree that a real material-structural world exists, and that an aspect of that real world is the existence of conscious conceptualizing humans. (ii) They agree that highly structured material reality must exist prior to conscious human ideas, theory and culture. (iii) They agree that structured material reality can continue to exist without conscious human ideas, theory or culture, but not vice versa. (iv) They agree that the content and structure of material reality is initially, i.e., in the primary stages of each emerging moment, very significant in providing the dominant material-structural data out of which human existence and experience must be constructed and to which it must, to a great degree, conform; this is accounted for in the category of efficient causation in Whitehead's theory, and in the first premises of the materialist method in Marx (GI 42). (v) They agree that conscious humans develop, intentionally and unintentionally, ideas, theory and culture which may conform or not conform to the structured material world. That is to say, a concept may be true or false, depending on its accuracy in reflecting reality; or a concept may be a "non-conformal proposition" of what is not but might be--both of which are verifiable through praxis. (vi) They agree that, in the context of a society, human ideas, theory and culture are a real force, i.e., "final-cause" or "material-force," and thus one of the abstract, but real, inter-related variables which must be considered in social theory. (vii) And they agree that for humans consciously to direct their own history, conscious theoretical work is very important because, although in itself theory does not change our material, structural and cultural existence which is the foundation of our human existence and experience, in the human context as we know it, it (theory) can be a real force. And more importantly, without ideas and theory there is not praxis, only response and unintentional creation of the present and future human society. Thus there is extensive theoretical agreement between Marxist theory and Whitehead on this issue.

Radical divergence, on the materialist-idealist question, comes at the point where the process theory, as developed by Whitehead, posits "eternal objects" and theology. The concept eternal is part-of Whitehead's process scheme and even though it does not in fact apply to complex ideas or propositions, which are historical in Whitehead's scheme, the category eternal like materialism provides a linguistic and conceptual stumbling block because if either material or idea (form, in this case) have an eternal or ontological primacy, we are back with a materialist-idealist problem. In this instance Whitehead is a metaphysical-idealist, and even though the notions of the eternalness of forms and of God are derivative in nature (PR 46), and of little significance for the application of the process paradigm to social theory, they provide the greatest problem for consonance between Whitehead and Marxist theory, and for a paradigm shift from materialism to process. A solution would be the development of a process model based on Process and Reality which excluded the derivative notions of God and of the eternalness of forms.

I discuss the possibility of a paradigm shift, and a resolution of the materialist-idealist question even in light of the last paragraph, obviously not because there are no problems with Whitehead's process model, but because it seems to me that (i) Marxist theory in many ways is a process-relational model in need of relational concepts and language, which could be provided by the concepts of process and "actual event", and (ii) the process model is not fundamentally altered (i.e., it does not cease to be a process model) if the eternalness of forms and their place of residence, i.e., God, are removed. On the other hand, if the "materialist" model is modified to be a process-relational model, it ceases to be a "materialist" model conceived in terms of causal primacy. And even though in its overall analysis and conclusions Marxist theory (if it were to make such a shift) would not radically change its language and conceptual images would change and thus no longer by definition invite a materialist-idealist discussion, except of course, from those who, having studied the theory, said it was incorrect either because (i) they held material-structural reality to be the realization of eternal ideas, or God's plan, or (ii) they held consciousness, ideas, theory and culture to be simply the function of material-structural reality.[5] Upon careful reading there are very few social theorists who hold either of these latter positions. But admittedly for these theorists the materialist-idealist question would still exist in some form.

2. Implications for the Freedom-Determinism Question in Marxist Theory

The freedom vs. determinism problem is posed (i) by the mechanistic and thus non-freedom implications of such statements as, "it is not the consciousness of men that determines their existence, but their social existence that determines their consciousness [Critique 21]," (ii) by the non-freedom associated with the terms materialism and behaviorism, and (iii) by the implication in liberalism that causation is limited to human action. This latter position is exemplified in such statements as "things do not act, only persons act"; a statement which though usually attributable to personalists or humanists, can also be attributed to Marx. He writes:

> Nature builds no machines, no locomotives, railways, electric telegraphs, self-acting mules etc. These are products of human industry; natural material transformed into organs of the human will over nature, or of human participation in nature. They are organs of

145

the <u>human brain</u>, <u>created by</u> the human <u>hand</u>; the
power of knowledge, objectified   [<u>Grundrisse</u>
706].

It is significant that both the first and last statements
are written by Marx and neither of them is a unique or
isolated example. The problem is (i) that both statements
are true, if understood in conjunction with the other,
(ii) that neither is true in isolation, and finally (iii)
that the statements are either overstated in each case or
his conceptual or linguistic scheme is inadequate to
handle what he is trying to say. Ollman in <u>Alienation</u>
argues that Marx is a relational thinker and that is why
his (Marx's) words can mean different things at different
times, and why he can appear to make contradictory statements.[6] Furthermore he argues that if Marx is studied with
the assumption that he is a relational thinker then he will
no longer appear contradictory, or mechanistic in terms of
his statements which refer to causation. I am inclined to
agree with Ollman, not because of the argumentation of his
book (which I find overstated), but because it was not
until I had studied Whitehead's <u>Process and Reality</u> that
I began to feel I understood what Marx was writing.[7]
Whether or not Marx's theoretical work and social analysis
accurately and helpfully describe human social reality
is, of course, a debated question; I have implicitly
argued in Chapter II that they do. However, the work of
Althusser, Habermas and Ollman, all contemporaries, bear
witness to the fact that Marx can be understood differ-
ently, particularly on the issue of freedom and determinism.[8]

      In Chapters I and II, I discussed subjective freedom
in Whitehead and Marxist theory. In both theories subjective will or freedom is a significant factor when
placed in the context of the other forces of existence.
Although, significantly, in Marxist theory there is no
systematic exposition of the various aspects of causation
or the nature of the causal character of physical and
social (non-human) realities; thus when he (Marx) writes
that existence <u>determines</u> consciousness, or that "the
handmill gives <u>you</u> society with the feudal lord; the
steam-mill, society with the industrial capitalist [PP
109]," one might conclude (i) that things and social
structures are attributed with what we normally consider
"human-will", (ii) that human will and consciousness have
been stripped of any autonomy or self-direction and humans
are defined as <u>simply</u> functions of their material-structural existence, or (iii) that both of the above are true.
There are at least three ways of avoiding the pitfall of

misunderstanding Marx in one of these, above listed, ways. First one can read Marx extensively and balance his comments over against each other, choose a mid-point, and conclude that he doesn't really mean those absolute statements in the way that they sound, or they need to be understood in context--this approach will solve many of the problems. Second, one can take the Ollman approach, which is to say that Marx was really a relational thinker, and thus the reader must understand that Marx is writing from that perspective. The third alternative would be to read Marx's theory extensively and in context, i.e., both in his historical context and statements in their full literary context. And instead of attributing a relational paradigm to Marx (which is difficult, because although he frequently uses relational categories, he expressly defined his method as materialist), I suggest that the reader him/herself make the paradigm shift to a relational model and then approach the freedom-determinism question in Marxist theory from that perspective. That is to say, I suggest the reader read Marx through relational glasses.

Recall from Chapter I that causation in the process paradigm has three distinct aspects or modes; (i) efficient causation, i.e., the throbbing vector force of the actual material, structural and cultural environment, (ii) final causation, i.e., the luring force of ideas, forms and beliefs which have been inherited from the social environment or subjectively created, and (iii) self-causation or subjective aim, i.e., the capacity of the emergent individual subject to influence his/her own present experience and his/her own character as super-ject. These forms of causation are independent inter-related abstract forms of determination which by definition (in the process paradigm) presuppose each other. The implications of reading Marx's theory with this perspective include these: If Marx presents a discussion of the influence of existence on the subjective consciousness and will, and on culture, religion, etc., he can be understood as presenting the arguments for the reality of efficient causation, or more accurately we can understand that the realities described can be accounted for via the category of efficient causation without being required to project a relational model onto Marx, and without being caught in the freedom-determinism problem. This is possible because it can be assumed that examples and affirmation of efficient causation do not exclude final and self-causation, i.e., examples and affirmation of the determinant influence of existence on consciousness and culture are true without being inclusive of truth. For example it can be argued that in Boston the existence of medicines, equipment and hospitals and health care personnel, arranged primarily in a structure of private ownership of material and skills, and a free-for-service delivery system, have a determinant influence on (i) culture, e.g., the maintenance of the belief that health care is not a human right, but something for which you contract and purchase, and (ii) human decisions, e.g., the simple choice to use the facilities, since they are there, or the influencing of health care personnel to work, and health care facilities to be placed where there is the greatest remuneration rather than the greatest need.[9] Or finally those persons with less money and therefore less access to health care will "choose" to seek health care less often than the wealthier, if for no other reason than that their priority for food, shelter, etc., will be relatively higher since they spend a higher percentage of their income for food and housing.

When Marx writes that theory can become a material force when it has seized the masses (CHR 52), that ideas function conservatively as the ruling ideas of the ruling classes (GI 64-65), or that social knowledge becomes a direct force of production (Grundrisse 706); or if we simply acknowledge the valuative and judicial power of concepts such as "alienation", "exploitation", and "one-sided crippled development" (GI 105-06); he (Marx) can be understood as presenting the arguments for the reality of "final causation." Or more accurately we can understand that the realities described can be accounted for via the category of "final causation" without being required to project the category onto Marx, and without being caught in the freedom-determinism problematic, because it can be assumed that examples and affirmation of "final causation" do not exclude "efficient" and "self-causation", i.e., examples and affirmation of the determinant influence of ideas upon conscious will and existence are true without being inclusive of truth. For example it can be argued that the type, location, and structure of health care and delivery in Boston, and a whole range of subjective decisions related to children's access to health care in Boston are influenced by the following: (i) the belief in private ownership and disposition of material property and acquired knowledge and skills, (ii) the idea of a contract between freely consenting individuals,[10] and (iii) the theory that public ownership, financing and distribution of commodity or services limits personal freedom.[11] On the other hand it can be argued that the belief that access to health care is a human right, is a growing force, and that that belief is seizing or taking hold of people in Boston, particularly where its appeal is

148

ad hominem.

Finally when Marx writes, for example, that human will can transform nature (Grundrisse 706), that "man makes his life activity itself an object of his will and consciousness [EPM 127]," or that the life-process of society should be "treated as production by freely associated men, and . . . consciously regulated by them in accordance with a settled plan [Capital I 80, my emphasis]," he (Marx) can be understood as presenting the arguments for the reality of "self-causation," or more accurately, we can understand that the realities described can be accounted for via the category of "self-causation" without being required to project the category onto Marx, and without being caught in the freedom-determinism question, because it can be assumed that examples and affirmation of the "self-causation" do not exclude "efficient" or "final" causation, i.e., examples and affirmation of the determinant influence of the "subjective will" choosing and creating ideas and theories, and acting upon material and structural reality are true without being inclusive of truth. For example, I discussed in Chapter I the human capacity consciously to entertain conformal and non-conformal propositions, e.g., "the children in Boston have access to free health care." I also discussed the human capacity to choose this proposition as desirable for actualization, to further analyze the whole situation and to put into propositional form the necessary material, structural and cultural changes which would be necessary for that non-conformal proposition to be actualized. This is the importance of the human capacity to theorize (also discussed in Chapters I and II). It can further be argued and demonstrated that humans in Boston have the capacity to act, and to change the material, structural and cultural conditions in such a way as to move in the direction of actualizing the experience desired for Boston children. The propositions (theory) which are providing direction for the willed action, and the content of the action itself, are complex, changing and directional, i.e., they move toward the goal through praxis, in which process, the goal itself may change. As Marx noted so emphatically in Poverty of Philosophy (191ff) and The Holy Family (127ff), both the propositions (theory) and human willed action are necessary, but it is the changed material, structural, and cultural conditions which will determine whether or not the children in Boston experience free access to health care.

The concern of the last few pages is to demonstrate how, if we make a paradigm shift to a process model, we can understand, learn from, and utilize Marxist theory without being burdened by the freedom-determinism question because if Marx's categories and discussions of the determining influence of the various factors of society (i.e., material, structures, culture and human will) are not understood as discussion of exclusive or sole determinant factors, but as aspects of a processing whole (organic or not), then we have by-passed the categorical problem of whether-or-not ideas and things act, and humans are free.

3. Implications for the Epistemological Question in Marxist Theory

The problem may have two facets; the first being whether or not there is a real world out there, and the second, if there is, how do we learn or come to know anything about it and how do we know that what we know accurately describes it.

Both Whitehead and Marxist theorists start with the assumption that there is a real world of which human persons are an emergent aspect.[12] Marx's theory of knowledge follows from this assumption and, as we noted in Chapter II, is a "non-philosophical" (philosophical here meaning conceived abstractly apart from experience) position that we gain knowledge of the world through our sense perceptions, knowledge which is verified in life praxis[13] and testified to by the status of natural science and modern industry. Lenin and Mao deal more systematically with the question of knowledge, but they only elaborate and do not change the theory. Lenin, in response to an idealism which denies or at least does not know if there is anything-in-itself, argues throughout Materialism and Empirio-Criticism[14] (i) that the real world exists whether or not it is known, (ii) that mental images are reflections or pictures of reality and not "derived by thought out of itself,"[15] and (iii) that verification comes through practice. Lenin writes:

> Thus, the materialist theory, the theory of reflection of objects by our mind, is here presented with absolute clarity: things exist outside us. Our perceptions and ideas are their images. Verification of these images, differentiation between true and false images, is given by practice.[16]

Mao's epistemology is essentially the same; read again the last sentence of his essay "On Practice":

> The discovery of truths through practice, the verification and the development of them through practice, the active development of perceptual knowledge into rational knowledge and, by means of rational knowledge, the active direction of revolutionary practice and the reconstruction of the subjective and the external world--practice, knowledge, more practice, more knowledge, and the repetition ad infinitum of this cyclic pattern, and with each cycle, the elevation of the content of practice and knowledge to a higher level--such is the epistemology of dialectical materialism, such is its theory of the unity of knowledge and action.[17]

Here Mao speaks not only of verification through praxis, but of a previous step, i.e., the development of perceptions into rational knowledge. This is a process he refers to earlier when he distinguishes between sensation and conceptualization:

> . . . the sensations and images of a thing are repeated innumerable times, and then a sudden change in the cognitive process takes place, resulting in the formation of concepts. Concepts as such no longer represent the external aspect of things, their individual aspects, or their external relations. Through concepts man comes to grasp a thing in its entirety, its essence, and its internal relations.[18]

With this passage from Mao we are very close to Whitehead's process model. That is to say, if we draw upon our discussion of Whitehead in Chapter I, we can understand a Marxist epistemology to include the following: (i) there is a real world, aspects of which are organic, of which one complex emergent aspect is sensuous humans, who in their individual-character are externally related to the rest of reality, (ii) perceptions or conscious sensations, are individual images or reflections which (iii) through repetition of sensation, and action/practice based on those sensations, gain verification, and arrangement or organization in consciousness, i.e., what Mao refers to above as "conceptualization" and what Whitehead terms "propositional form." (iv) These "concepts" (or theories or propositions) are the complex theories which become for Marxists the theoretical aspect of praxis.

Mao's notion of conceptualization is a considerable contribution to that of Marx and Lenin, and Whitehead's development in Process and Reality fleshes out this model even further. Whitehead's process model begins with the same premise as the Marxists, i.e., with the one world and the emergence of sensuous humanity, internally related to that world. But in Whitehead's scheme, sensation, feeling or prehension, in their most primitive or simplistic form are pre-conscious and are the direct actual link with the outside world, i.e., an aspect of internal-relatedness and the source of direct knowledge or "conceptual repro- duction" in the pre-conscious Whiteheadian sense. White- head's second phase of knowledge, i.e., conceptual reversion, which is the first stage of selection and arrangement is also pre-conscious. It is not until the third phase, i.e., transmutation, that the plethora of sensations, directly felt, selected, sorted, and ar- ranged, become an organized mental construct and emerge in consciousness as the images or reflections (to which Lenin refers) which to a greater or lesser degree accurately reflect the rocks, trees, people, etc., as distinct en- tities. Yet another stage of mental organization must take place before the images are as Mao writes, grasped in their "entirety," "essence" and "internal relations" or arranged in conceptual (Mao) or propositional (Whitehead) form.

The most advanced phase of the epistemological struggle, i.e., revolutionary praxis, is of course more developed in the Marxist model than in Whitehead or process theory in general. It should be noted however that the praxis motif is operative throughout in both episte- mological schemes.

In the first instance Whitehead and Marxist theo- rists begin with a common assumption of a real world of which humans are an emergent and internally related part, thus in this sense Whitehead adds nothing to Marxist theory. However, in the above discussion I have attempted to demonstrate that Whitehead can make a contribution to the Marxist epistemological discussion at two points. First Whitehead develops (as an aspect of the whole paradigm) an explicit notion of internal relations, which is implicit in much Marxist theory but not explicitly developed in Marxist theory, albeit attributed to it by Ollman. Second and more importantly for the epistemo- logical question, Whitehead provides an accounting for conscious conceptual mistakes in a paradigm which has humans directly and internally related to the rest of reality. And he does this in a way which is consonant with Marxist materialism, but without the materialist language, that is to say, although Whitehead probably did not read Lenin, his (Whitehead's) analysis is consonant with, but goes beyond, such statements as this by Lenin:

> For every scientist . . . as well as for every materialist, sensation is indeed the direct connection between consciousness and the external world; it is the transformation of the energy of external excitation into a state of consciousness.[19]

Whitehead's scheme goes beyond this by presenting a scheme which places error not between the external world and sensation, but between sensations (i.e., feelings or prehensions which are primary and direct) and complex conscious images constituted from a selection and arrangement of sensations which have been "transmuted" from the medium of direct communication, i.e., "feeling" and sensation, to conscious image; as Whitehead notes, "perception is cognition of prehension [SMW 71]." It is thus in the selection (and exclusion), arrangement and transmution of sensations (i.e., a process of abstraction) into conscious images and conceptions or propositions, that error enters; it is thus (as far as epistemology is concerned) not the human being which is externally related to the rest of reality, but it is that high level aspect of humanness, i.e., conceptual consciousness which is not only the epitome of individuality, but has the quality of externality to the senses. I emphasize conceptual consciousness because much, if not most, of human experience, including consciousness, is at the level of feeling and not conceptuality.[20]

Thus Marxists and Whitehead agree that the world is real and that we have direct sense-knowledge of that world. And it is in the cognition or interpretation of the sense perception that we can account for error and verification.

This is particularly applicable for social theory, and it underscores the importance and force of ideology and world view, for as I discussed in Chapter I, our inherited and chosen beliefs select, organize and transmit many of our sensations (at the pre-conscious level) to images and concepts at a conscious level. Thus for example, two individuals with different ideologies may

observe the same Boston health-care situation different-
ly. One may conceptualize the gradual destruction of good
medical care and human freedoms because of government
regulation and creeping socialism, and the other may
conceptualize a misuse of resources and a maldistribution
of health care due to a fee-for-service delivery system
and a monopolization of medical knowledge by a few. That
is to say, how the epistemological question is resolved
will have its effect on social theorists who wish to
explain theoretically why _facts_ mean different things to
different people.

In conclusion, unlike the questions of idealism vs.
materialism and freedom vs. determinism, on the question
of epistemology, Whitehead does not so much offer a
helpful paradigm shift as an elaboration and a fuller
development of Marxist theory.

B. Possible Implications for
Actualizing Conscious Intervention

1. Implications of "Quality of Subjective
Experience" and the "Social Nature of Humans"
Linked with "Human Development" as the Normative
Referent

I have discussed in Chapter I and II the empirically
derived theoretical understanding of the nature (historical and emergent, not metaphysical)[21] of reality, including humanity, for Whitehead and for Marxist theory. I
have also discussed how these understandings of the nature
of reality provide something of a functioning normative
referent for evaluating material, structural and cultural
existence, and for guiding conscious intentional
change.[22] I.e., Whitehead emphasized (i) the value of the
quality of subjective personal experience and (ii) the
social and relational character of all reality including
humans. The Marxist theoretical reference is akin to
this, but is more singularly expressed as the overcoming
of human alienation (from one's productive activity,
one's product, others, and the species)[23] and the development of the powers and capacities of species individuals.

I want to suggest that Whitehead's developed theory
can benefit Marxist theory in this area, on two points:
(i) Whitehead locates in his concern for the quality of
pre-conscious and conscious subjective experience, the
precise, albeit abstract, moment, place or locus of value,
i.e., the raison d'etre for any kind of development, or

conscious intervention in the historical process toward that end. (ii) Whitehead in <u>Process and Reality</u>, in his emphasis on the (ontological) social nature of all reality, and his moving within one paradigm back and forth on the continuum from realities such as a moment in the duration of a stone's existence to the non-conformal proposition of human consciousness, locates humanity explicitly in the natural world and thus provides no rationale for a human versus nature dualism (in which, for example, nature exists for the sake of human appropriation);[24] but provides rather a theoretical rationale for reciprocal relationship between all aspects of nature.

Marxist theory is concerned with the quality of human experience; e.g., the category "alienation" in Marxist theory describes at once a material and structural reality, and a quality of pre-conscious and conscious experience. Furthermore, placing the locus of value in experience in no way detracts from the importance and accuracy of the Marxist conclusion that high quality experience <u>requires</u> an environment of enabling and compatible material, structural and cultural factors. Whitehead's developed theory, however, does add clarity as to the locus of value, for human social theory, as well as proposing the understanding that "subjective experience" is an aspect of all reality, albeit, of much greater significance and intensity in higher organisms such as humans. The point to be made here is that <u>if</u> the locus of value is subjective experience, <u>and</u> subjective experience is a characteristic of reality; <u>then</u> it follows that social theorists who wish consciously to intervene in the process of history, out of an awareness of the nature of reality, will not make the categorical distinction between humans and nature that is implicit in much of Marxist theory, and they will have a theoretical referent which maintains a focus on the value of the individual. This in no way detracts from the importance of the species-character of humans nor does it provide an immediate solution to the perpetual problem of the good of one versus the good of the many; although this latter problem is significantly reduced in intensity by understanding reality as social in nature and humans as species in character.

We have noted that in both Marxist theory and Whitehead, reality is social in nature, and that humans are an emergent creative aspect of the reality.[25] Marxist theory however posits a hierarchical and nonreciprocal distinction between <u>nature</u> and <u>humans</u>.[26] For example, Marx in general affirms the change in the relation between humans and nature, brought about by capitalism, i.e.,

> For the first time, nature becomes purely an
> object for humankind, purely a matter of utili-
> ty; ceases to be recognized as a power for
> itself; and the theoretical discovery of its
> autonomous laws appears merely as a ruse so as
> to subjugate it under human needs, whether as
> an object of consumption or as a means of
> production [Grundrisse 410].

Ollman also reflects this perspective when he writes:

> In its most general sense, 'appropriation'
> means to utilize constructively, to build by
> incorporating; the subject, whether stated or
> implied, is man's essential powers. For Marx,
> the individual appropriates the nature he per-
> ceives and has become oriented to by making it
> in some way a part of himself with whatever
> effect this has on his senses and future orien-
> tation.[27]

Nature thus exists _for_ human use, that is to say, the
relationship between nature and humans is subordinate and
not reciprocal. This is apparent in what Ollman accurately writes: "Marx presents alienation as partaking of four
broad relations which are so distributed as to cover the
whole of human existence. These are man's relations to his
productive activity, his product, other men, and the
species."[28]

Notice that these relations listed do not include
the relationship between humans and the rest of nature.
That humans as a species have an internal, and reciprocal
relationship with our natural environment, a relationship
which is also subject to radical alienation is graphically
demonstrated by the massive ecological issues which face
us now, and will increasingly in the future. These are
issues which are concerned with such basic internal relationships between individual humans and the natural
environment, as the oxygen we breathe and burn every
second of our lives. As Marx so astutely pointed out there
is more than a utility relationship between individual
humans and (i) other humans, (ii) their productive activity, and (iii) the products of their labor; in like
manner, there is more than a utility relationship between
humans and the rest of nature.

The absence, in Marxist theory, of an emphasis on
this issue should be corrected, and it can be by (i) taking
seriously the social nature of reality, (ii) overcoming

the dualism of humanity versus the rest of nature, and (iii) by applying the paradigm of process and internal relations to the relationship between humans and nature. In this sense Whitehead's paradigm as developed in Process and Reality could go beyond and facilitate a correction of this weakness in the humanism of Marxist theory. If Whitehead's process paradigm were applied to Marxist theory it would require a social theory which would be socialist not only in terms of human and productive relations, but also in terms of human-nature relations. This follows necessarily from Whitehead's theory of the individual as a "social reality" in the context of the continuum of nature.[29]

In this context then, the implications of Whitehead's theory for persons who take Marxist theory seriously and who wish to intervene consciously in the process of history are, (i) that the normative referent of overcoming human alienation and of enabling human development will be sharpened by understanding the locus of value to be the quality of subjective experience and (ii) that subordinate-utilitarian status of the rest of nature to the human species will be qualitatively changed by an inclusive interpretation and application of the social nature of reality. The first of these changes could facilitate subtle but significant changes in perspective, for example, under a normative referent which called for development of human capacities, the delivery of health care to children in hospitals can be mechanistically geared to (i) saving lives, (ii) correcting dysfunctions, (iii) curing "cases," etc. If the referent included the quality of subjective experience, not only would the items listed receive attention as prerequisites, but these experiences (for everyone involved) would be viewed not only as means to health or human development, but also as ends-in-themselves. This is the existential quality which is found developed in the process paradigm and implicit in the Marxist concept of alienation. The second of these implications is a major shift, not only for Marxist theory; because most if not all western social theory is consonant with the Genesis command for humans to fill the earth, subdue it and take dominion over all living things in the sea, on the land, and in the air.[30] The industrialized countries of the West and East are now driving to its conclusion this real and theoretical relation of human exploitation of nature. But in this conclusion is revealed the falseness, i.e., destructiveness of the relation. If humans continue to relate to their ecological environment in an exploitative rather than a reciprocal, relational manner, the species may well suffocate itself.

An example of a possible implication of this perspective is, for persons who wish to intervene consciously in the process of history, to see pollution, not just as a danger to health, but as alienating to human existence, as is the commoditization and selling of human labor power. Thus as we seek to change structures of production, not necessarily to increase production but to decrease alienation and to increase the quality of subjective experience, so a process theory would require that we alter our destruction of nature not only to raise the level of physical health, but also to decrease the alienation between the species and nature. This is in no way a mystical statement; it is rather an attempt to understand and to include in theoretical categories a very real, i.e., material, structural and cultural experience of alienation.

2. Implications of Minimal Influence on the Present and Significant Influence on the Future

In Chapter I, we discussed, that according to Whitehead's scheme, an experience is nearly complete before consciousness emerges, that is to say, that consciousness is a very high level and late phase of any actual event which reaches consciousness; thus a conscious person has very little capacity to influence the content and form of any present experience. Furthermore I discussed that to be a significant influence consciously in the flow and process of history a person must influence the late phase of the present in such a way that the present becomes the desired determinant past for the future. It is in the late phase of concrescence that conscious will gains its power and influence by including conceptual and physical data in that occasion and thus giving that data objective determinant status for the future. This is, of course, a statement about each moment in a process and therefore it is an on-going and emergent process. For example, the experience today of children in Boston purchasing health care is the product of past production of goods, training of personnel, passing of laws, structuring of the economic, social and political relations, affirmation of cultural values, etc. If we wish the experience of the children in Boston to be different we must, in the present, begin the process of material, structural, and cultural changes which will create the necessary determinate and determinant past for that future experience. This is the time lag factor which I will discuss at greater length below.

Marxist theory does not provide a systematic theoretical explanation of how it is true on the one hand that social existence determines consciousness and on the other hand that consciously willed action determines or can determine social existence.[31] Both of these affirmations are true, but from Marxist theory we get no theoretical framework by which to make them mutually supportive, rather than apparently contradictory. The affirmation in Marx is clear: "If man is shaped by his surroundings, his surroundings must be made human. If man is social by nature, he will develop his true nature only in society, . . . [HF 176]." And one theoretical scheme for how it is that the men/women who are perpetually shaped by their surroundings, can in the same process perpetually and consciously shape their surroundings and thus their future selves, is provided by applying Whitehead's process paradigm to Marxist theory. It is here that I find the significance of the discussion, in Chapter I, which concluded that humans have little influence on the form and content of experiences which are already conscious experiences, and the capacity for great influence on the future. Marxist theory and Whitehead agree that our material, structural and cultural social environment has determinant influence on who we are and what we experience. Whitehead accounts for this with the category of efficient causation.

Marxist theory puts great stress on the fact that it is action and not the entertaining of ideas which will change the form, content and thus the quality of experience. Marxist theory however implicitly and explicitly affirms that it must be the right action, i.e., it must be informed by correct ideas or theory. Whitehead does not put the emphasis on action--it is only implicit in Whitehead--but his discussion of the emergence of consciousness and the conscious capacity for entertaining conformal and non-conformal propositions, and the capacity to choose which propositions to include as definitive of the late phase of that moment's concrescence, gives a theoretical framework for understanding how a socially shaped Marxist consciously transcends his existence, and develops non-conformal theory which does not significantly change his/her immediate social existence or experience, but which does define and give direction to his/her present action in such a way that it is intentional intervention in the material, structural and cultural present, for the future.

A very significant concept here is that of the negative judgment and non-conformal proposition, i.e., the capacity of conscious humans (whose existence and consciousness is inherited or brought forth from, the relevant social environment) to entertain conceptually what is not, from the exclusiveness of what is. This is how the socially determined human who does theory for the future can be understood. In Whitehead as in Marxist theory, theory does not significantly influence the present; it does not significantly influence anything until it is actualized, i.e., given material as well as conceptual reality. In this sense Whitehead is as much a materialist as Marx, with the exception that Whitehead is more systematic, not only in explaining the emergence of non-conformal theory, but also in consistently maintaining the reciprocal relationship between conceptual and material reality.

For clarification I can abstract several elements from the process I have been discussing. Existence: We begin with our determinate and determinant material, structural and cultural environment from which we emerge and which provides almost all of the data for our experience. Subjective experience: The quality of subjective experience is of primary concern to social theorists who are concerned to understand experience in such a way that they not only understand its origin, nature, form and content but in a way which enables the control and changing of experience. Theory: Our theoretical efforts discover that the present occasion which we are experiencing is already in an advanced stage and nearly complete; its material, structure and ideas inherited from its social environment are of necessity in a very advanced complex arrangement before consciousness emerges. But the theoretical effort also discovers that conscious humans can consciously and theoretically transcend existence, i.e., human consciousness can (building on what is given in the social environment) experience conceptually that which is not actual, or found in the social environment. The theoretical effort also discovers that subjective persons have a minimal capacity to consciously will and choose the conceptual and material content for the late phase of that experience. Subjectively willed action: We can will and actualize minimal material, structural and cultural changes in our emergent existence, which when actualized and past, will be the determinate and determinant data for the future. Changed environment: The willed actions, when actualized are thus a changed social environment, which in effect changes the existence of emergent occasions in the relevant future and thus it is these future moments of experience whose quality of experience is most significantly effected by willed action in their relevant past. There is thus a necessary lag time between (i) conceptualizing a desirable experience, (ii) willing and actualizing the necessary material, structural and cultural changes, and (iii) the emergence of an occasion whose determinant social environment reflects those changes, and which thus inherits the material, structural and cultural data necessary to <u>bring forth</u> the desired experience. The present can leave a significantly modified social environment when it changes from the present to the past, but the present must actualize, i.e., move into its superjective character before there is a changed environment from which a new occasion with the desired experience can emerge.

If for example one or a group of persons were to observe the status of health of Boston children, they might conclude among other things that many of the children are not as healthy as they might be. If this person or persons were evaluating the situation from either a Marxist or process perspective they would assume that the state of health of the children is a function of the children's material, structural and cultural environment, and to a limited degree of the subjective freedom of the individuals involved. The last factor is affirmed, but is not a variable which can be controlled. It then would be assumed that if the might be, i.e., the experience of a higher level of healthiness, were to become an actuality, it would necessitate some theoretical description of what experience was desired and a decision as to what material, structural and cultural changes in the social environment would bring forth that experience. This theory and action would then become a praxis movement toward the desired experience, that is to say, action would be taken and changes made, the results and then the theory re-examined and so on until the desired experience is experienced at some later time.

The point of the example is three-fold: (i) The status of health and the experience of healthiness, in general is a function of the actual material, structural and cultural environment, and cannot be changed unless there are actual changes in that environment. (ii) That social environment which is determinant of the status of the experience of healthiness is created originally and perpetually by humans in a reciprocal relation with it, that is to say, in one sense it is a product of human activity, and thus it can be changed by human activity. (iii) Humans do not have the capacity to will changes instantaneously, either in the quality of their experience or in the content and form of their social environment, but they do have the capacity consciously to transcend their experience and existence, and to understand the nature of the process and to initiate changes which will bring forth a significantly different kind and/or quality of experience in the future.

Bowles and Gintis, in their discussion of class power, make essentially the same point as I try to make with the above example. They write:

> . . . people control their personal development by progressively tailoring their social environment to their manifest needs through their conscious wills. A sphere of social life will be called integrated[32] if the social institutions and power relations of this sphere facilitate the translation of human needs into social outcomes through individual choice and collective action. When a sphere of social life (e.g., education, work, community) is integrated, it develops historically in conformity with the developmental needs of individuals. The transformed social environment, by satisfying these needs and creating a consciousness of further needs, thus creates the conditions for its further transformation and development. In an integrated setting, personal development and the development of the social environment proceed hand in hand.[33]

Once it is understood that humans have the capacity to significantly influence the process in the present for the future, that this is an emergent on-going process and that the really significant results are only in the future, and only as a result of the actual material, structural and cultural changes; then the importance of the compatibility of factors within the environment and particular types of experience is again in the foreground.

3. Implications of the Concept of Compatibliity

In analyzing any situation, a materialist model—by definition—begins with the material-structural conditions. That is to say, the materialist model puts great importance upon the force of the material-structural existence to influence the type and quality of experience. From a process perspective, we can understand this to come under the category of efficient causation, with the exception that materialists usually exclude from efficient causation the existent culture, i.e., beliefs, ideas, theories, etc. And any discussion of change therefore focuses on the change of material-structural conditions which are assumed to be primary and fundamental.

Idealists and cultural theorists are more inclined to begin with, and continue to focus upon, the importance of culture, i.e., belief systems, theories, world views, etc. They are concerned with the power which belief systems have for holding and directing human societies; a power which in the process model is termed final causation. Within the cultural perspective a discussion about increasing the quality, or changing the type of experience, will focus on the cultural belief system, and conclude that the first step is to get the correct ideas and beliefs, and all else will follow.[34] This position is exemplified in religious traditions which emphasize credal positions, and by cultural anthropologists, to the extent that they emphasize the cultural aspects of society as independent variables.[35]

I will also mention the subjectivist perspective which begins with, and continues to focus upon human free will and subjectivity as the only active force in social reality; subjective will is understood here as transcendent over material things and ideas which are inert material and tools for the creative will.[36] This position finds expression (i) in philosophical and social theory which does not go beyond the statement, "things do not act, only people act," (ii) in much of modern psychology which locates problem and solution, not in the material-structural conditions in which persons live, and generally not in the belief systems by which people are held, and (iii) to some degree in fringe movements which focus on the power of positive thinking, or various forms of meditation. This emphasis is accounted for in the process model by the category of subjective aim.

It can be said from a process perspective that there is truth in each of these perspectives but that it is to commit the fallacy of misplaced concreteness to identify any of these factors as an independent variable, or as the primary independent-interdependent variable.

If there is a contribution to be made by process theory to this aspect of social theory it is first in its emphasis on a balanced inter-relatedness of the various factors[37] and types of causation, and second, in its related focus upon compatibility rather than on any primary factor; that there is primary (efficient), causation

is true, but all factors (except the subject), are effective via this mode of causation. The concept of compatibility here means that if a particular type and quality of
experience is desired, the social environment, from which
that experience must come forth must be compatible with
the desired experience. For example, the experience of
free access to health care for the children in Boston is
probably incompatible with a social environment which
includes (i) a fee-for-service delivery system and a legal
monopoly of medical authority by medical doctors, (ii) a
legal structure and belief system which does not define
equitable access to health care as a human right, and (iii)
a geographical distribution of facilities and personnel
according to distribution of wealth rather than population and need.

"Social environment" is used here in a Whiteheadian
sense, and thus includes the ecological environment,
technology, social structures and culture. The social
environment can be abstractly broken down into various
different lists of abstract factors; the important thing
is (i) that the list is inclusive, (ii) that it facilitates
understanding of the dynamic social process, and (iii)
that it reveals loci where leverage for intentional change
can be applied.

When discussing compatibility and social environment it may be helpful to reread Whitehead's statement in
Process and Reality:

> Every actual entity is in its nature essen-
> tially social; and this in two ways. First, the
> outlines of its own character are determined by
> the data which its environment provides for its
> process of feeling. Secondly, these data are
> not extrinsic to the entity; they constitute
> that display of the universe which is inherent
> in the entity. Thus the data upon which the
> subject passes judgment are themselves compo-
> nents conditioning the character of the judging
> subject. It follows that any general presuppo-
> sition as to the character of the experiencing
> subject also implies a general presupposition
> as to the social environment providing the
> display for that subject [PR 309].

The concept of compatibility thus moves the concentration away from a primary focus on (i) material (efficient causation), (ii) ideas or culture (final causation),
or (iii) subjective will (self-causation) and begins with

the assumption of these abstract and interrelated foci, and focuses on the content and arrangement of the material and culture of the social environment. For it is assumed from this perspective that the whole social environment is important and that if a certain type of experience is desired, its prerequisite social environment must be created.

> . . . the presupposed or desired type of enti-
> ties requires a presupposed type of data for
> the primary phases of these actual entities;
> and . . . a presupposed type of data requires
> a presupposed type of social environment [PR
> 311].

This notion is not new; Marx made the point over and over again in his view that advanced science and technology are necessary to enable human life to get beyond drudgery and to a higher plain of freedom where humans do not have to work full time in material production for food and shelter. He also made the point when he said that certain modes of production brought forth certain types of social and cultural existence.[38] But what is different in the process concept of compatibility is (i) that the dialectic between foundation and superstructure--not the dialectic between theory and practice--is replaced by a dynamic (but lawful) reciprocal causation between the various internally related factors, and (ii) that no factor or factors are by definition primary.

A criticism of this approach is that it can have a tendency to degenerate into a study of equal independent-interdependent factors, with each factor gaining its own field of study, e.g., economics, political science, sociology, psychology, etc. If the distinction and importance of the three modes of causation are not maintained, the question of compatibility can become a sort of sociology of interacting, equal and independent variables. Such a change would indeed change Marxist theory from a theory for revolutionary change into a Marxist "sociology." An excellent criticism of this approach is written by Korsch.[39] He writes that the problem of a Marxist "sociological tendency" is that it supplants

> . . . the basic importance of the production-
> relations for all political, legal, ideologi-
> cal phenomena occurring in a given socio-eco-
> nomic formation by a "co-ordination" of the
> "interactions" going to and fro between the
> various departments of social life and, ulti-

mately, by a "universal interdependence of all social spheres." The materialistic conception of history, then, no longer appears as the principle of a materialistic science investigating all facts of history from the point of view of their specific relation to material production. It appears at its best as a general empirical and positivistic method which represents all facts in their own contexts and not in connection with any preconceived "idea" at all.[40]

His discussion is certainly a criticism of a "departmentalizing" tendency. On first reading, it also appears as a criticism which makes this discussion of compatibility a destructive "watering process" which "impairs the scientific utility to the scheme [Marxism] itself," because it replaces the "materialist principle."[41] Korsch's argument is very cogent, but the process perspective survives his criticism because the materialist principle of causality is not simply replaced by reciprocal interaction between independent variables,[42] or by the absence of lawful causality in general, but by a reaffirmation of the importance of social environment along with a coherent inclusion of final and self-causation which are also affirmed by Marx, albeit in a non-schematic way.

Marxists such as Korsch are frequently required to explain away the "assumed one-sidedness of Marxian materialistic conception of history," (i) as the unavoidable generalizations of theoretical statements (Korsch, p. 223), or (ii) with the affirmation that Marx was really writing out of a world view based on internal relations.[43] While there is significant cogency in both arguments, there is a common denominator for these two arguments and this discussion on the implications of compatibility in process theory, for Marxist theory. And that common denominator is Marxist theory itself, that is to say, while Marxist theory is compelling in its analysis and conclusions, and has proven useful in facilitating revolutionary change, the language and structure of its presentation require interpretation or translation to make it holistic and coherent. And it can be argued that any such interpretation or translation--be it Korsch's, Ollman's or this study's--is something of an addition or modification. It is with this awareness and in the context of an appreciation for both the qualities and limitations of Marxist theory, and the categories of process theory, that I have discussed the possible implications of compatibility (and process theory in general), for Marxist theory.

C. Summary

In summary I can point to the following implications of Whitehead's understanding for Marxist theory.

(i) Whitehead has developed a process-relational scheme which in general gives credence to the possibility of relational thinking, and in particular provides a developed referent with which to understand and judge the possibility of a relational world view being the real motif of Marx's writing.

(ii) If Marxist theory were to make a paradigm shift from "materialism" to "process," its overall analysis and conclusions would not radically change, but its language and conceptual images would change in such a way as no longer to invite a materialist-idealist discussion, that is to say, the relevant category "actual event" is inclusive of the variables which are at odds in a materialist-idealist discussion.

(iii) The process categories of efficient, final, and self-causation provide an effective means of discussing causation in a systematic way which is inclusive of the determinant character of social existence and culture, and also of subjective will; thus by-passing the freedom-determinism question by affirming each real force in its time, place and character, in a complementary not paradoxical fashion.

(iv) Whitehead's developed theory can assist Marxists epistemologically by systematically explaining how direct sensation, feeling or perception, is selected, abstracted and transmuted before it is experienced consciously. Thus the epistemological question of error is accounted for within a scheme which affirms a direct relationship with the real world.

(v) The normative referent of overcoming human alienation and of enabling human development will be sharpened by understanding the locus of value to be the quality of subjective experience. Whitehead's emphasis on the social nature of reality drives Marxist theory beyond its traditional man vs. nature "humanism," and toward a socialism which includes the relationship of the species to the rest of nature.

(vi)   The explanation of consciousness as a late
phase of concrescence, with its greatest capacity for
intervention being the changing of the present for the
future, provides a theoretical scheme which accounts for
and makes mutually supportive, the dual affirmation that
social existence determines consciousness and that consciously willed action can determine social existence. It
also accounts for the necessary time lag between the
willing of an experience, the changing of the social
environment, and the emergence of an occasion which will
have the willed experience.

(vii)   The concept of compatibility moves the focus
away from a primary focus on material and structural
efficient causation.   It begins rather with material,
structural, cultural and subjective reality interacting
lawfully via the three modes of causation and focuses on
the content and arrangement (i.e., structuring) of the
material, structures and culture of the social environment. For in light of the three modes of causation, it is
assumed in this perspective that the whole social environment is important and that if a certain type of experience is desired, its prerequisite social environment must
be created.

Chapter III - Notes

1. See for example Needham's <u>Order and Life</u>; his presentation is consonant with a process-relational view on two important points: (i) methodologically,

> "It is to be noted that the new conception of biological organization combines the insistence of vitalism on the real complexity of life with the heuristic virtues of the mechanistic practical attack [p. 9]."

And (ii) the theory that the qualitatively new and the unique are viewed not as the product of "some supra-material" factors, but rather of "stages of complexity" in the organization of a material complex (p. 165). See also pp. 25-26.

2. Harris, <u>Rise of Anthropological Theory</u>, p. 231.

3. For an excellent statement of this problem, and its potential resolution, in anthropology, see Clifford Geertz, "Ritual and Social Change: A Javanese Example," <u>American Anthropologist</u>, LIX (1957), pp. 32-54.

4. It has already been noted (Introduction: section on Limitations) that this rests on my interpretation of Marxist theory and is limited to the problem of this study.

5. Harris' "techno-environmental and techno-economic determinism" or "cultural materialism" is as deterministic as any theory which I have read, and even he would not argue that consciousness, ideas, theory and culture are simply the function of material-structural reality. Harris, <u>The Rise of Anthroplogical Theory</u>, see pp. 4, 231, 244f, & 659.

6. See Ollman's chapter "With Words That Appear Like Bats," in <u>Alienation</u>, pp. 3-11.

7. And it is equally the case that I didn't see the importance of the ontological principle and efficient causation for general social theory until I had studied Marx.

8. Althusser argues for an accent on <u>materialism</u> found in an emphasis on the post-1850s writings of Marx. Habermas and Ollman both prefer the earlier writings, with Habermas taking a very psychologically oriented humanistic perspective and Ollman, of course, arguing for a relational interpretation with causation being understood as <u>reciprocal relations</u>.

9. See for example, S. Wolfe, "Primary Health Care for the Poor in the United States and Canada," <u>International Journal of Health Services</u>, Volume 2, Number 2, pp. 218ff.

10. Milton Friedman in Capitalism and Freedom (Chicago: University of Chicago Press, 1962), presents a chapter on "Occupational Licensure," pp. 137-60, in which he acclaims not only the "triumph of ideas" (p. 137), but also the idea of a free contract in the area of medical care delivery. For example he writes: "Insofar as he [the doctor] harms only his patient, that is simply a question of voluntary contract and exchange between the patient and his physician. On this score, there is no ground for [government] intervention [p. 147]."

11. Ibid., especially pp. 178-89.

12. Lenin, Materialism and Empirio-Criticism, pp. 63-64; Whitehead, Process and Reality, pp. 161-167; and Needham, "A Biologist's View of Whitehead," pp. 264-66.

13. Lenin, Materialism and Empirio-Criticism, pp. 99f, 106, 136 & 142.

14. Ibid., see for example, pp. 33f, 38, 63 & 191.

15. Ibid., p. 33.

16. Lenin, Materialism and Empirio-Criticism, p. 106.

17. Schram, Political Thought of Mao Tse-tung, p. 194, my emphasis.

18. Ibid., p. 191.

19. Lenin, Mateialism and Empirio-Criticism, p. 44.

20. Maurice Merleau-Ponty in The Structure of Behavior translated by Alden L. Fisher (Boston: Beacon Press, 1963, c1942), especially pp. 189-224, deals with consciousness, its emergence into the world and the question of epistemology from the perspective of a phenomenological-structuralism which is in many ways similar to Whitehead's perspective. For example he writes, p. 189, "the body forms a screen between us and things." Or again, p. 190, "Perception will result from an action of the thing on the body and of the body on the soul." See also especially p. 199. Furthermore on pp. 201ff, he discusses "the dialectic of the epistemological subject and the scientific object," in a way which appears to be functionally the same as the praxis motif in Whitehead and Marx.

21. Recall Marcuse's statement quoted in Chapter II:
    "Truth, in short, is not a realm apart from historical reality, nor a region of eternally valid ideas. To be sure, it transcends the given historical reality, but only in so far as it crosses from one historical state to another." Marcuse, Reason and Revolution, p. 315.

22. The deriving of a normative referent from knowledge of the nature of reality is also discussed by Joseph Needham in Time: The Refreshing River (London: George Allen & Unwin Ltd., 1943). For example he writes p. 55:

"Perhaps the most important task before scientific thinkers today is to show in detail how the ethics of collectivism do in fact emerge from what we know of the world and the evolutionary process that has taken place in it. Scientific socialism (I believe) is the only form of socialism which has the future before it; its theoreticians must therefore show not only that high levels of human social organization have arisen and will arise by a continuation of the natural process, but what are the ethics appropriate to them." See also "The Biological Basis of Sociology," pp. 160-77.

23. Ollman, Alienation, p. 137.

24. See Ollman's chapter on "Appropriation" in Alienation, pp. 91ff for a good example of this dualism in Marxist theory.

25. As Parsons, in "History as Viewed by Marx and Whitehead," p. 289, accurately writes: "On this our two philosophers are agreed: the history of men depends on the men of history, acting within the objective conditions of past history and the universe of nature." See also p. 284, where he writes of the agreement between Marx and Whitehead on the fact that "man comes out of nature and in turn shapes his environment."

26. This is a difficult point, because I do not want to say that there is no distinction between humanity and nature. I affirm with both Marx and Whitehead that there is a quantitative difference which is significant enough to make a qualitative difference. As Needham in Time: The Refreshing River, p. 243, says so well: "It would be correct to say that the living differs from the dead in degree and not in kind because it is on a higher plane of complexity of organization, but it would also be correct to say that it differs in kind since the laws of this higher organization only operate there." I emphasize the continuity of nature and humanity in this section in an effort to speak to the condition of alienation between men/women and nature.

27. Ollman, Alienation, p. 91.

28. Ibid., p. 137.

29. See Sullivan, "The Process Social Paradigm and the Problem of Social Order," especially p. 21.

30. Genesis 1:28f.

171

31. Elements for such a theoretical explanation built on Marxist theory, can be found in Mannheim's _Ideology and Utopia_. See especially pp. 29, 47f, 186 & 248.

32. The term "integrated" as used here is very similar to the term "compatible"; this should be kept in mind while reading the next section of this chapter.

33. Samuel Bowles and Herbert Gintis, "Class Power and Alienated Labor," _Monthly Review_ 26 (March 1975), p. 12.

34. This is one of the viewpoints that Marx saw and criticized in Proudhon. See _Poverty of Philosophy_, p. 191.

35. Interestingly, _Adventures of Ideas_, in isolation, is a good example of this perspective.

36. For an example of this position see Browning, "Whitehead's Theory of Human Agency," p. 437. For Browning, the human agent must somehow be able to "act" in a way which is transcendent of, or at least not a "sub-process of concrescence." David Bidney's "personalistic, organic, humanistic theory of culture", as developed in his _Theoretical Anthropology_ (2nd augmented ed.; New York: Schocken Books, 1953), especially pp. 137 and 104, is another good example of this perspective.

37. Merleau-Ponty in _The Structure of Behavior_ proposes a naturalism (which is phenomenological, structural and holistic), which also attempts to get beyond the divisions of mechanism, finalism and mentalism, for example he writes p. 184,
    "Aided by the notion of structure or form, we have arrived at the conclusion that both mechanism and finalism should be rejected and that the 'physical,' the 'vital' and the 'mental' do not represent three powers of being, but three dialects. Physical nature in man is not subordinated to a vital principle, the organism does not conspire to actualize an idea, and the mental is not a motor principle _in_ the body; but what we call life is already consciousness of life and what we call mental is still an objective vis-a-vis consciousness."
See also especially his section on "Naturalism" pp. 201-20.

38. Marxists must also be credited with being much more outspoken and progressive in their criticism and action against alienating and unfulfilling social conditions than was Whitehead or process theorists in general.

39. Korsch, _Karl Marx_, pp. 218-28.

40. _Ibid._, p. 218.

41. Ibid., p. 223.

42. Ollman comes very close to this position in Alienation, see for
example p. 131. To avoid this pitfall, a relational model requires
an explication of causation which is scientific in the sense that it
enables not only understanding, but also a degree of prediction and
intervention.

43. Ollman, Alienation.

CHAPTER IV

CONCLUSION

In this final chapter I will review the process of the study, review the major findings of the study and summarize my conclusions.

A. Review of the Process

I began this study by defining a limited and specific problem to be addressed. This specific problem was to analyze the category of consciousness as developed in Alfred North Whitehead's philosophy of organism, and to explore critically the possible contribution of Whitehead's analysis to Marxist theory at the point where Marxist theory deals with the capacity of humans to intervene creatively and consciously in the process of history. I noted that I understand Marxist theory to be an unfinished and still developing theory and that because of this I would not seek to either find or define a normative "Marxist theory" but rather I would use a method which included Marx's writings and a sample of writings from Marxist theorists which represents the range of "Marxist theory" on the categories and issues relevant to the problem of this study. The method for approaching Whitehead's philosophy was different. This is for two reasons. First, because Whitehead's cosmology and developed theoretical scheme is developed systematically in one book (Process and Reality) and thus this one work became the primary source--to be supported by other writings by Whitehead and his students--for this study. The second reason is that this study is concerned with Whitehead's philosophical categories as he developed them and with Marxist theory as it is developing and emerging.

The study is structured into an Introduction, three substantive chapters and this Conclusion. The three substantive chapters are structured so that the first of them is concerned with Whitehead's theory, the second with Marxist theory, and the third with defining problem areas in Marxist theory which can be addressed by the process theory as developed in Whitehead. The third chapter therefore--by definition--points out divergences between Whitehead's theory and Marxist and Marxist theory; while in both Chapter II and II there are references to areas of compatibility between the theories.

B. Review of the Major Findings

In Chapter I, when discussing Whitehead's theoretical understanding of consciousness in the context of the problem of the human capacity consciously to intervene in history, I found the following categories and concepts to be important.

(i) The nature of reality is social and the locus of experience is the subjective individual. This dual affirmation follows directly from the ontological principle and the three modes of causation, that is to say, the ontological principle asserts a relational, i.e., social, world view, and the three modes of causation are not isolated independent forms of causation but abstract concepts which illuminate forms of causation within one relational, i.e., social, world. But it is also that--for Whitehead--it is only in the subjective aspect that there is experience and that therefore that is where there is value, and furthermore that as the quality of that subjective experience--located as it is in a social and causal world--increases, so value increases.

(ii) I found that conscious information of our contemporary and historical world is possible via presentational immediacy, and that knowledge of the caused, and thus predictable, process is possible when empirical research and imagination--controlled by coherence and logic--are aided by inductive reason and generalization.

(iii) I found that conscious persons have the capacity to make negative judgments, create and believe non-conformal propositions, and selectively include, exclude and arrange the physical and conceptual data of the late phases of their immediate experience; and by so doing they can have some influence on their immediate subjective experience and great influence on their relevant future.

(iv) I found that persons when making these decisions for the future, must deal with value questions and with questions of compatibility of variables. The value questions are the questions of what type and intensity of subjective experience is desired for individuals, and the compatibility questions have to do with determining the characteristics of the social--material, structural and cultural--environment which is necessary, if not sufficient, for the desired experiences.

These are the major findings of Chapter I of the study. And while I referred to them occasionally in

Chapter II, to illustrate parallels with Marxist theory, these findings were for the most part held in abeyance until Chapter III when I discussed them in relation to their possible contribution to Marxist theory.

Chapter II on Marxist theory provided me with these findings which are relevant to this study.

(i)   The materialist   method of   Marxist theory, premised on a holistic--non-dualistic--world view, finds the nature of reality to be social.

(ii) Marxist theory finds that human individuals in society are <u>natural</u>, <u>social</u>, <u>historical</u>, and <u>species</u> in character. Their species-nature has two aspects, viz., the species-relationship between individuals, and self-consciousness.

(iii) I found that the implicit historical goal of human history, in Marxist theory, is the development of species-individuals' powers and capacities. By inference, or derivatively, I concluded that the locus of value in Marxist theory is species-individuals, i.e., humans.

(iv)   I found that according to Marxist theory, conscious information and knowledge of our contemporary and historical world is possible through conceptualization of, and empirical testing of, sense perception; as demonstrated in natural science and the development of industry. Knowledge of the world and society is also revised and corrected by theoretical and practical criticism of existing theories and actual situations.

(v)   While again it is not systematically developed, I did find in Marxist theory, by implication and examples, that conscious persons have the capacity subjectively to transcend their existence, to theorize, and to develop new ideas and theory. These ideas, however, find their force only in giving direction or incentive to human practical activity which can in turn change the material structural conditions in which species-individuals are productive and reproductive.

(vi)   In this context I found that human activity, to be effectively human, must be socially organized and rationally planned, i.e., for the future, in response to knowledge of the nature of reality, and past activity and experience.

(vii) Finally, when making planning decisions for the future of society, species-individuals must deal with the implicit normative referent of the development of human powers and capacities, and with questions of the compatibility between that referent and certain types of material, structural and cultural environments.

By comparing the findings from Chapter I with those from II I find a great deal of similarity and consonance. Both have a holistic world view which is social, i.e., relational, in nature. And while Whitehead is more systematic in his presentation I find that both theories account for the determinant influence of the material, social and cultural environment, as well as that of subjective will and consciously created propositions or theory. Furthermore there seems to be similarity between the theories as to when, how and with what limitations, conscious humans effectively intervene in their own historical process. This similarity is a logical and necessary result of the fact that both theories operate from a premise/conclusion of the social nature of reality and the locus of value--or normative referent--being the subjective individual. The implication of this combined perspective is of course that the development of certain types of subjective individuals or experiences cannot be done instantaneously but requires the prior development of a compatible social environment.

The development and awareness of these basic similarities is important for showing the extent of the consonance between the two groups. I pointed out this consonance throughout Chapters II and III in order to provide background and context for pointing out problem areas in Marxist theory and exploring possible ways that Whitehead's theory may contribute to Marxist theory.

With the exception of Whitehead's theology and the "eternal" character of his "eternal objects," the divergencies between Marxist theory and Whitehead's philosophy of organism are not as fundamental as the similarities (with reference to the problems of this study). Nonetheless they are there and they are important, as I attempted to demonstrate in Chapter III. The purpose of this whole study however was neither to demonstrate the general consonance or dissonance between Whitehead's paradigm and Marxist theory, but rather to explore the areas in which Whitehead's theory might contribute to Marxist theory. When I discussed the parallels it was for this end.

It is in Chapter III where, drawing on the analyses and conclusions of Chapters I and II, I identified the relevant problem areas in Marxist theory and brought Whitehead's theory to bear on them. The major findings of Chapter III are as follows:

(i)   Whitehead has developed a process-relational scheme which in general gives credence to the possibility of relational thinking, and in particular provides a developed referent with which to understand and judge the possibility of a relational world view being the real motif of Marx's writings.

(ii) If Marxist theory were to make a paradigm shift from "materialism" to "process," its overall analysis and conclusions would not radically change, but its language and conceptual images would change in such a way as no longer to invite a materialist-idealist discussion, that is to say, the relevant category "actual event" is inclusive of the variables which are at odds in a materialist-idealist discussion.

(iii) The process categories of efficient, final and self-causation provide an effective means of discussing causation in a systematic way which is inclusive of the determinant character of social existence and culture, and also of subjective will; thus by-passing the freedom-determinism question by affirming each real force in its time, place and character, in a complementary, not para-doxical fashion.

(iv) Whitehead's developed theory can assist Marxists epistemologically by systematically explaining how direct sensation, feeling or perception, is selected, abstracted and transmuted before it is experienced consciously. Thus the epistemological question of error is accounted for within a scheme which affirms a direct relationship with the real world.

(v)   The normative referent of overcoming human alienation and of enabling human development will be sharpened by understanding the locus of value to be the quality of subjective experience. Whitehead's emphasis on the social nature of reality drives Marxist theory beyond its traditional man vs. nature "humanism," and toward a socialism which includes the relationship of the species to the rest of nature.

(vi) The explanation of consciousness as a late phase of concrescence, with its greatest capacity for intervention being the changing of the present for the future, provides a theoretical scheme which accounts for and makes mutually supportive, the dual affirmation that social existence determines consciousness and that consciously willed action can determine social existence. It also accounts for the necessary time lag between the willing of an experience, the changing of the social environment, and the emergence of an occasion which will have the willed experience.

(vii) The concept of compatibility moves the focus away from a primary focus on material and structural efficient causation. It begins rather with material, structural, cultural and subjective reality interacting lawfully via the three modes of causation and focuses on the content and arrangement of the material, structures and culture of the social environment. For in light of the three modes of causation, it is assumed in this perspective that the whole social environment is important and that if a certain type of experience is desired, its prerequisite social environment must be created.

C. Conclusions

I have been concerned in this study with problem areas in Marxist social theory at the point where Marxist social theory struggles with the human capacity to intervene consciously in the process of human history. I have explored relevant categories in Whitehead's philosophy of organism. I have explored and discussed the relevant categories and perspectives in Marxist social theory and illustrated areas of compatibility between Whitehead's theory and Marxist theory. Finally I have identified problem areas in Marxist theory and explored the possible ways Whitehead's theory may contribute to clarifying, bypassing and/or resolving these problems. I conclude from this process that there are divergent aspects between the theories, that Marx may not have been a "relational" thinker, and that it would not be a constructive project to replace Marxist theory with process theory, nor to advocate that Marxists change their categorical framework. I have concluded that there is a great deal of consonance between the two theories. And finally I have concluded that an understanding of, and identification with, Whitehead's world view and categories will facilitate a clearer understanding of Marxist theory and a more efficient utilization of that theory by those who wish to use it for understanding and intervening in the process of history.

Appendix 1

Engels' 1890 Letter to Joseph Bloch
(Marx and Engels, Selected Correspondence, pp. 475-77)

According to the materialist conception of history the determining element in history is ultimately the production and
reproduction in real life. More than this neither Marx nor I
have ever asserted. If therefore somebody twists this into the
statement that the economic element is the only determining one,
he transforms it into a meaningless, abstract and absurd phrase.
The economic situation is the basis, but the various elements of
the superstructure--political forms of the class struggle and
its consequences, constitutions established by the victorious
class after a successful battle, etc.--forms of law--and then
even the reflexes of all these actual struggles in the brains of
the combatants: political, legal, philosophical theories,
religious ideas and their further development into systems of
dogma--also exercise their influence upon the course of the
historical struggles and in many cases preponderate in determining their form.   There is an interaction of all these
elements in which, amid all the endless host of accidents (i.e.,
of things and events, whose inner connection is so remote or so
impossible to prove that we regard it as absent and can neglect
it) the economic movement finally asserts itself as necessary.
Otherwise the application of the theory to any period of history
one chose would be easier than the solution of a simple equation
of the first degree.
    We make our own history, but in the first place under very
definite presuppositions and conditions.   Among these the
economic ones are finally decisive.   But the political, etc.,
ones, and indeed even the traditions which haunt human minds
also play a part, although not the decisive one. . . .
    In the second place, however, history makes itself in such a
way that the final always arises from conflicts between many
individual wills, of which each again has been made what it is
by a host of particular conditions of life.   Thus there are
innumerable intersecting forces, an infinite series of paral-
lelograms of forces which give rise to one resultant--the
historical event.
· ·
    Marx and I are ourselves partly to blame for the fact that
younger writers sometimes lay more stress on the economic side
than is due to it.   We had to emphasize this main principle in
opposition to our adversaries, who denied it, and we had not
always the time, the place or the opportunity to allow the other

elements involved in the interaction to come into their rights.*

-- Selsam, et al., <u>Dynamics of Social Change</u>, pp. 76-79

Althusser's position in the criticism is essentially the one Engels is trying to counter. His criticism is weak at several points: (i) Althusser criticizes one small abstracted segment of the letter, in his long appendix, while in the remainder of his essay (109-16), he affirms the position of Engels' letter, e.g., just before he affirmatively quotes a long segment of Engels' letter (112), he writes: "However Marx has given us the 'two ends of the chain', and has told us to find out what goes on between them: on the one hand, <u>determination in the last instance by the</u> (economic) <u>mode of production</u>; on the other, <u>the relative autonomy of the superstructures and their specific effectivity</u> [111]." (ii) Althusser accuses Engels of reflecting the <u>ideology</u> of "a world which would be reducible to its essence: The conscious will of individuals, their actions and their private undertakings [126-27]." Such an accusation cannot come from reading Engels' letter; and therefore must reflect what Engels would call the "undialectic," or dualistic position which Althusser poses when he sets the issue as "individual wills" <u>vs.</u> "quite simply . . . the Marxist solution [124]", which for him is "determination <u>by the</u> economy <u>in the last</u> instance [125]." Neither Engels nor Marx posited conscious human wills as independent of their existence, but neither were they reductionist to economic factors. (iii) And perhaps most paradoxical is that both Engels in his letter and Althusser in his introduction to <u>For Marx</u> refer to the importance of theory, yet Althusser in his criticism doesn't even acknowledge the presence of the category in Engels' letter, nor the significant implication of Engels' and Althusser's works, i.e., the historical dialectical, reciprocity between (i) <u>material conditions</u>, (ii) theorizing, i.e., conscious, reflecting, willing, acting <u>humans</u>, and (iii) developed theory.

Althusser, however, does seem to affirm this dialectic in the last section of his essay (109-16); it is thus somewhat mystifying why he takes the position which he does in his long appendix.

For a criticism of the Engels' "self-criticism" letter, from a perspective which is more akin to Althusser's, usually theoretical, position, see Korsh, <u>Karl Marx</u>, pp. 221-24.

*Note: Althusser in <u>For Marx</u>, pp. 117-28, provides a long criticism (in the form of an appendix), of a portion of this letter by Engels.

Appendix 2

Engels' 1893 Letter to Franz Mehring
(Marx and Engels, <u>Selected Correspondence</u>, pp. 510-12)

There is only one other point lacking, which, however, Marx and I always failed to stress enough in our writings and in regard to which we are all equally guilty. We all, that is to say, laid and were bound to lay the main emphasis at first on the derivation of political, juridical and other ideological notions, and of the actions arising through the medium of these notions, from basic economic facts. But in so doing we neglected the formal side--the way in which these notions come about--for the sake of the content.

. . . .

Hanging together with this too is the fatuous notion of ideologists that because we deny an independent historical development to the various ideological spheres which play a part in history we also deny them any effect upon history. The basis of this is the common undialectical conception of cause and effect as rigidly opposite poles, the total disregarding of interaction; these gentlemen often almost deliberately forget that once a historic element has been brought into the world by other elements, ultimately by economic facts, it also reacts in its turn and may react on its environment and even on its own causes.

-- Selsam, et al., <u>Dynamics of Social Change</u>, pp. 72-74.

Appendix 3

Engels' 1894 Letter to Heinz Starkenburg
(Marx and Engels, Selected Correspondence, pp. 516-19)

We regard economic conditions as the factor which ultimately determines historical development. But race is itself an economic factor. Here, however, two points must not be overlooked:

(a) Political, juridical, philosophical, religious, literary, artistic, etc., development is based on economic development. But all these react upon one another and also upon the economic base. It is not that the economic position is the cause and alone active, while everything else only has a passive effect. There is, rather, interaction on the basis of the economic necessity, which ultimately always asserts itself. . . . So it is not, . . . that the economic position produces an automatic effect. Men make their history themselves, only in given surroundings which condition it and on the basis of actual relations already existing, among which the economic relations, however much they may be influenced by the other political and ideological ones, are still ultimately the decisive ones, forming the red thread which runs through them and alone leads to understanding.

(b) Men make their history themselves, but not as yet with a collective will or according to a collective plan . . .

-- Selsam, et al., Dynamics of Social Change, p. 75.

Appendix 4

Gramsci on the Nature of Man/Woman

Possibility means "freedom". The measure of freedom enters into the concept of man. That the objective possibilities exist for people not to die of hunger and that people do die of hunger, has its importance, or so one would have thought. But the existence of objective conditions, of possibilities or of freedom is not yet enough: it is necessary to "know" them, and know how to use them. And to want to use them. Man, in this sense, is concrete will, that is, the effective application of the abstract will or vital impulse to the concrete means which realize such a will. Men create their own personality, 1. by giving a specific and concrete ("rational") direction to their own vital impulse or will; 2. by identifying the means which will make this will concrete and specific and not arbitrary; 3. by contributing to modify the ensemble of the concrete conditions for realizing this will to the extent of one's own limits and capacities and in the most fruitful form. Man is to be conceived as an historical block of purely individual and subjective elements and of mass and objective or material elements with which the individual is in an active relationship. To transform the external world, the general system of relations, is to potentiate oneself and to develop oneself. That ethical "improvement" is purely individual is an illusion and an error: the synthesis of the elements constituting individuality is "individual", but it cannot be realized and developed without an activity directed outward, modifying external relations both with nature and, in varying degrees, with other men, in the various social circles in which one lives, up to the greatest relationship of all, which embraces the whole human species. For this reason one can say that man is essentially "political" since it is through the activity of transforming and consciously directing other men that man realizes his "humanity", his "human nature".

-- Gramsci, Prison Notebooks, p. 360.

Appendix 5

Marx on the Nature of Man/Woman
(Marx, "Excerpt-Notes of 1844")

Suppose we had produced things <u>as</u> <u>human</u> <u>beings</u>:* in his production each of us would have <u>twice</u> <u>affirmed</u> himself and the other. (1) In my <u>production</u> I would have objectified my <u>individuality</u> and its <u>particularity</u>, and in the course of the activity I would have enjoyed an individual <u>life</u>; in viewing the object I would have experienced the individual joy of knowing my personality as an <u>objective</u>, <u>sensuously</u> <u>perceptible</u>, and <u>indubitable</u> power. (2) In your satisfaction and your use of my product I would have had the <u>direct</u> and conscious satisfaction that my work satisfied a <u>human</u> need, that it objectified <u>human</u> nature, and that it created an object appropriate to the need of another <u>human</u> being. (3) I would have been the <u>mediator</u> between you and the species and you would have experienced me as a redintegration of your own nature and a necessary part of your self; I would have been affirmed in your thought as well as your love. (4) In my individual life I would have directly created your life; in my individual activity I would have immediately <u>confirmed</u> and <u>realized</u> my true <u>human</u> and <u>social</u> nature.

Our productions would be so many mirrors reflecting our nature. What happens so far as I am concerned would also apply to you.

-- Easton and Guddat eds., <u>Writings of the Young Marx</u>, p. 281.

*My emphasis on these three words; remainder of the emphasis in the text.

Appendix 6

Production as Process

The conclusion we reach is not that production, distribution, exchange and consumption are identical, but that they all form the members of a totality, distinctions within a unity. Production predominates not only over itself, in the antithetical definition of production, but over the other moments as well. The process always returns to production to begin anew. That exchange and consumption cannot be predominant is self-evident. Likewise, distribution as distribution of products; while as distribution of the agents of production it is itself a moment of production. A definite production thus determines a definite consumption, distribution and exchange as well as definite relations between these different moments. Admittedly, however, in its one-sided form, production is itself determined by the other moments. For example if the market, i.e. the sphere of exchange, expands, then production grows in quantity and the divisions between its different branches becomes deeper. A change in distribution changes production, e.g. concentration of capital, different distribution of the population between town and country, etc. Finally, the needs of consumption determine production. Mutual interaction takes place between the different moments. This [is] the case with every organic whole [Grundrisse 99-100].

Appendix 7

Economic Relations as Process

It must be kept in mind that the new forces of production and relations of production do not develop out of <u>nothing</u>, nor drop from the sky, nor from the womb of the self-positing Idea; but from within and in antithesis to the existing development of production and the inherited, traditional relations of property. While in the completed bourgeois system every economic relation presupposes every other in its bourgeois economic form, and everything posited is thus also a presupposition, this is the case with every organic system. This organic system itself, as a totality, has its presuppositions, and its development to its totality consists precisely in subordinating all elements of society to itself, or in creating out of it the organs which it still lacks. This is historically how it becomes a totality. The process of becoming this totality forms a moment of its process, of its development [<u>Grundrisse</u> 278].

Appendix 8

Labor as Realization Process

Objectified labour ceases to exist in a dead state as an external, indifferent form on the substance, because it is itself again posited as a moment of living labour; as a relation of living labour to itself in an objective material, as the objectivity of living labour (as means and end [Objekt]) (the objective conditions of living labour). The transformation of the material by living labour, by the realization of living labour in the material—a transformation which, as purpose, determines labour and is its purposeful activation (a transformation which does not only posit the form as external to the inanimate object, as a mere vanishing image of its material consistency)—thus preserves the material in a definite form, and subjugates the transformation of the material to the purpose of labour. Labour is the living, form-giving fire; it is the transitoriness of things, their temporality, as their formation by living time. In the simple production process—leaving aside the realization process-the transitoriness of the forms of things is used to posit their usefulness [Grundrisse 360-61].

Appendix 9

Human Development

This claim is based on a view of man's essence not as a consumer of utilities but as a doer, a creator, an enjoyer of his human attributes [4].

The power-maximizing principle . . . is based on the proposition that the end or purpose of man is to use and develop his uniquely human attributes or capacities. His potential use and development of these may be called his human powers. A good life is one which maximizes these powers. A good society is one which maximizes (or permits and facilitates the maximization of) these powers, and thus enables men to make the best of themselves.

It is important to notice that this concept of powers is an ethical one, not a descriptive one.

. . . .

The ethical concept of a man's powers . . . necessarily includes in a man's powers not only his natural capacities (his energy and skill) but also his ability to exert them. It therefore includes access to whatever things outside himself are requisite to that exertion. It must therefore treat as a diminution of a man's powers whatever stands in the way of his realizing his human end, including any limitation of that access [8-9].

. . . while men's human attributes might be variously listed, they could 'be taken to include the capacity for rational understanding, for moral judgment and action, for aesthetic creation or contemplation, for the emotional activities of friendship and love, and, sometimes, for religious experience'. And of course the capacity for transforming what is given by Nature is presupposed in this view of men as essentially a doer, a creator, an exerter of energy, an actor; this is broader than, but includes, the capacity for materially productive labour. . . . One might add the capacity for wonder or curiousity; . . . for laughter . . . for controlled physical/mental/aesthetic activity, . . .

The further assumption, which at first sight is a staggering one, is that the exercise of his human capacities by each member of a society does not prevent other members exercising theirs: that the essentially human capacities may all be used and developed without hindering the use and development of all the rest [53-54].

The other point to be noticed about the concept of human capacities is that their exercise, to be fully human, must be under one's own conscious control rather than at the dictate of another. This is required by the concept of human essence which holds that a man's activity is to be regarded as human only in so far as it is directed by his own design (an assumption as old as Aristotle's to logon echon). To say this is not of course to say that a man should refuse to acknowledge himself to be a social animal who can be fully human only as a member of society. It is rather to say that the rules by which he is bound should be only those that can be rationally demonstrated to be necessary to society, and so to his humanity. . . .

. . . .

Finally we should notice that this view of capacities and their development, . . . does not imply that society is only an impeding agent. It does not deny that society is also a positive agent in the development of capacities. It does not deny that every individual's human capacities are socially derived, and that their development must also be social. Human society is the medium through which human capacities are developed. A society of some kind is a necessary condition of the development of individual capacities [56-57].

-- Macpherson, <u>Democratic Theory: Essays in Retrieval.</u>

191

Appendix 10

Human Development Continued
(Marx, "Economic and Philosophical Manuscripts")

But it is easy indeed to say to the particular individual what Aristotle said: You are engendered by your father and mother, and consequently it is the coitus of two human beings, a human species-act, which has produced the human being. You see, therefore, that even in a physical sense man owes his existence to man. Consequently, it is not enough to keep in view only one of the two aspects, the infinite progression, and to ask further: who engendered my father and my grandfather? You must also keep in mind the circular movement which is perceptible in that progression, according to which man, in the act of generation reproduces himself; thus man always remains the subject.

. . . .

Since, however, for socialist man, the whole of what is called world history is nothing but the creation of man by human labour, and the emergence of nature for man, he, therefore, has the evident and irrefutable proof of his self-creation, of his own origins. Once the essence of man and of nature, man as a natural being and nature as a human reality, has become evident in practical life, in sense experience, the quest for an alien being, a being above man and nature (a quest which is an avowal of the unreality of man and nature) becomes impossible in practice. Atheism, as a denial of this unreality, is no longer meaningful, for atheism is a negation of God and seeks to assert by this negation the existence of man. Socialism no longer requires such a roundabout method; it begins from the theo-retical and practical sense perception of man and nature as essential beings. It is positive human self-consciousness, no longer a self-consciousness attained through the negation of religion: just as the real life of man is positive and no longer attained through the negation of private property, through communism. Communism is the phase of negation of the negation and is, consequently, for the next stage of historical develop-ment, a real and necessary factor in the emancipation and rehabilitation of man. Communism is the necessary form and the dynamic principle of the immediate future, but communism is not itself the goal of human development--the form of human society.

-- Bottomore, ed. Karl Marx: Early Writings, pp. 165-67.

SELECTED BIBLIOGRAPHY

Books

Althusser, Louis. _For Marx_. New York: Vintage Books, 1970.

Bidney, David. _Theoretical Anthropology_. 2nd. augmented ed.
    New York: Schocken Books, 1953.

Christian, William A. _An Interpretation of Whitehead's Metaphysics_.
    New Haven: Yale University Press, 1967.

Easton, Loyd D. and Guddat, Kurt H. Translators and editors,
    Writings of the Young Marx on Philosophy and Society. New York:
    Doubleday & Co.; Anchor Books, 1967.

Engels, Frederick. _Anti-Duhring_. New York: International
    Publishers, 1939; New World Paperbacks, 1972.

Friedman, Milton. _Capitalism and Freedom_. Chicago: University
    of Chicago Press, 1962.

Geertz, Clifford. _Islam Observed_. New Haven: Yale University,
    1968; Chicago; Phoenix Books, 1971.

Gramsci, Antonio. _Letters From Prison_. New York: Harper and
    Row, 1973.

_____. _Selections From the Prison Notebooks_. New York:
    International Publishers, 1971.

Habermas, Jurgen. _Knowledge and Human Interests_. Boston:
    Beacon Press, 1971.

_____. _Theory and Practice_. Beacon Press, 1973.

Hall, David L. _The Civilization of Experience: A Whiteheadian
    Theory of Culture_. New York: Fordham University Press, 1972.

Harris, Marvin. _The Rise of Anthropological Theory_. New York:
    Thomas Y. Crowell Company, 1968.

Johnson, Allison H. _Whitehead's Philosophy of Civilization_.
    New York: Dover Publications, Inc., 1962.

_____. _Whitehead's Theory of Reality_. New York: Dover
    Publications, 1962.

Kautsky, Karl. <u>Ethics and the Materialist Conception of History</u>.
Translated by John B. Askew. 4th ed. revised. Chicago: Charles
H. Kerr & Co., 1911.

Kline, George L., ed. <u>Alfred North Whitehead: Essays On His
Philosophy</u>. Englewood Cliffs, N.J.: Prentice-Hall, 1963.

Korsch, Karl. <u>Karl Marx</u>. New York: Russell & Russell, 1963.

_____. <u>Marxism and Philosophy</u>. London: NLB, 1970.

Leclerc, Ivor. <u>Whitehead's Metaphysics: An Introductory
Exposition</u>. London: George Allen & Unwin L.T.D., 1958.

Lenin, V.I. <u>Materialism and Empirio-Criticism</u>. New York:
International Publishers, 1927.

Lewis, John. <u>The Marxism of Marx</u>. London: Lawrence & Wishart,
1972.

Lowe, Victor. <u>Understanding Whitehead</u>. Baltimore: Johns
Hopkins University Press, 1968.

Lukacs, Georg. <u>History of Class Consciousness</u>. Cambridge,
Massachusetts: MIT Press, 1971.

MacIver, R.M. <u>Social Causation</u>. Boston: Ginn and Co., 1942.

Macpherson, C.B. <u>Democratic Theory: Essays in Retrieval</u>.
Oxford: Clarendon Press, 1973.

Mannheim, Karl. <u>Ideology and Utopia</u>. New York: Harcourt,
Brace & World, 1936.

_____. <u>Essays on the Sociology of Knowledge</u>. London:
Routledge & Kegan Paul LTD, 1952, 1972.

Marcuse, Herbert. <u>Reason and Revolution</u>. New York: Humanities
Press, 1954.

Marx, Karl. <u>Capital</u>. Volumes 1, 2 and 3. Translated from
the Third German Edition by Samuel Moore and Edward Aveling,
edited by Frederick Engels. New York: International Publishers, 1967.

_____. <u>The Civil War in France</u>. Moscow: Progress Publishers,
1974.

_____. Contribution to the Critique of Hegel's Philosophy of Right: Introduction, in Karl Marx: Early Writings. Translated and edited by T.B. Bottomore. New York: McGraw-Hill, 1964, pp. 41-57.

_____. A Contribution to the Critique of Political Economy. Edited by Maurice Dobb. New York: International Publishers; New World Paperbacks, 1970.

_____. Critique of the Gotha Programme. New York: International Publishers; Little Marx Library, 1966.

_____. Economic and Philosophical Manuscripts in Karl Marx: Early Writings. Translated and edited by T.B. Bottomore. New York: McGraw-Hill, 1964, pp. 67-194.

_____. The 18th Brumaire of Louis Bonaparte. New York: International Publishers; New World Paperbacks, 1963.

_____. Grundrisse: Foundations of the Critique of Political Economy. Translated by Martin Nicolaus. Middlesex, England: Penguin Books, 1973.

_____. Karl Marx: Selected Writings in Sociology and Social Philosophy. Translated and edited by T.B. Bottomore. New York: McGraw-Hill, 1956.

_____. On The Jewish Question in Karl Marx: Early Writings. Translated and edited by T.B. Bottomore. New York: McGraw-Hill, 1964, pp. 1-40.

_____. Poverty of Philosophy. New York: International Publishers; New World Paperbacks, 1963.

_____. These on Feuerbach, Karl Marx: Selected Writings in Sociology and Social Philosophy. Translated and edited by T.B. Bottomore. New York: McGraw-Hill, 1956.

Marx, Karl and Engels, Friedrich. Basic Writings on Politics and Philosophy. Edited by Lewis S. Feuer. New York: Doubleday, 1959.

_____. The German Ideology. Edited by E.J. Arthur. New York: International Publishers; New World Paperbacks, 1970.

_____. The Holy Family. Moscow: Foreign Languages Publishing House, 1956.

_____. "Manifesto of the Communist Party," in Marx, Karl and Engels, Friedrich. Basic Writings on Politics and Philosophy. Edited by Lewis Feuer. New York: Doubleday, 1959.

_____. On the Paris Commune. Moscow: Progress Publishers, 1971.

Merleau-Ponty, Maurice. The Structure of Behavior. Translated by Alden L. Fisher. Boston: Beacon Press, 1963, c1942.

Needham, Joseph. Order and Life. New Haven: Yale University Press, 1936; Cambridge: MIT Press, 1968.

_____. Time: The Refreshing River. London: George Allen & Unwin Ltd., 1948, c1943.

Ollman, Bertell. Alienation: Marx's Conception of Man in a Capitalist Society. Cambridge, England: Cambridge University Press, 1971.

Schilpp, Paul Arthur, ed. The Philosophy of Alfred North Whitehead. LaSalle, Illinois: Open Court, 1951.

Schram, Stuart R. The Political Thought of Mao Tse-Tung. Revised and Enlarged ed. New York: Praeger Publishers, 1969.

Selsam, Howard, Goldway, David, and Martel, Harry, eds. Dynamic of Social Change. New York: International Publishers, 1970; New World Paperbacks, 1973.

Sherburne, Donald W. A Key to Whitehead's Process and Reality. New York: Macmillan Co., 1966.

Sherburne, Donald W. A Whiteheadian Aesthetic. Handem, Connecticut: Archon Books, 1970.

Whitehead, Alfred North. Adventures of Ideas. New York: Macmillan, 1933; Free Press, 1967.

_____. The Function of Reason. Princeton: Princeton University Press, 1929; Boston: Beacon Press, 1958.

_____. Modes of Thought. New York: Macmillan, 1938; Free Press, 1968.

_____. Process and Reality. New York: Macmillan Company, 1929; New York: Harper Torchbooks, 1960.

_____. Science and the Modern World. New York: Macmillan, 1925; Free Press, 1967.

_____. Symbolism. New York: Macmillan, 1927; Capricorn Books, 1969.

Articles

Baldwin, Dalton D. "Evil and Persuasive Power: A Response to Hare and Madden." Process Studies, 3/4 (Winter, 1973): 259-283.

Barnhart, J.E. "Persuasive and Coercive Power in Process Metaphysics." Process Studies, 3/3 (Fall, 1973), 153-168.

Bennett, John B. "A Suggestion on 'Consciousness' in Process and Reality." Process Studies, 3/1 (Spring, 1972), 41-2.

Brennan, Sheilah O'Flynn. "Perception and Causality; Whitehead and Aristotle," Process Studies, 3/4 (Winter 1973): 273-83.

Bowles, Samuel and Gintis, Herbert. "Class Power and Alienated Labor," in Monthly Review, 26 (March 1975): 9-25.

Browning, Douglas. "Whitehead's Theory of Human Agency." Dialogue, 2/4 (1964), 424-41.

Geertz, Clifford. "Ritual and Social Change: A Javanese Example," in American Anthropologist. LIX (1957): 32-54.

"The Hungarian New Left: Sociology and Revolution," The Monthly Review (26 (April 1975): 33-47.

Leclerc, Ivor. "The Necessity Today of the Philosophy of Nature," Process Studies, 3/3 Fall, 1973: 158-68.

Needham, Joseph. "A Biologist's View of Whitehead's Philosophy," in Schilpp, Paul Arthur, ed. The Philosophy of Alfred North Whitehead. LaSalle, Illinois: Open Court, 1951.

Parsons, Howard L. "History as Viewed by Marx and Whitehead," Christian Scholar L (1967): 273-89.

Pixley, Jorge V. "Whitehead y Marx Sobre la Dinamica de la Historia." Dialogos 7 (April-June 1970): 83-107.

Sherburne, Donald W. "Whitehead Without God," Christian Scholar L (1967): 251-72.

Wolfe, S. "Primary Health Care for the Poor in the United States and Canada," International Journal of Health Services, 2/2, pp. 218ff.

Dissertations

Allan, George James. "A Whiteheadian Approach To The Philosophy of History." Unpublished Ph.D. dissertation, Yale University, 1963.

Cadwallader, Mervyn Leland. "A Cybernetic Theory of Social Change." Unpublished Ph.D. dissertation, University of Oregon, 1958.

Crocker, David Alan. "A Whiteheadian Theory of Intentions and Actions." Unpublished Ph.D. dissertation, Yale University, 1970.

DuBois, Ronald L. "Reason in Ethics: A Whiteheadian Perspective." Unpublished Ph.D. dissertation, St. Louis University, 1971.

Harrington, Michael Louis. "Whitehead's Theory of Propositions." Unpublished Ph.D. dissertation, Emory University, 1972.

Murphree, Wallace Allgood. "The Status of the Mental: A Whiteheadian Response to Armstrong's Materialism." Unpublished Ph.D. dissertation, Vanderbilt University, 1972.

Norris, Donald Carl. "A Critique of Whitehead's Theory of Consciousness." Unpublished Ph.D. dissertation, Boston University Graduate School, 1972.

Stevens, Edward Ira. "Freedom, Determinism, and Responsibility: An Analysis and A Whiteheadian Interpretation." Unpublished Ph.D. dissertation, Vanderbilt University, 1965.

Sullivan, William Michael. "The Process Social Paradigm and The Problem of Social Order." Unpublished Ph.D. dissertation, Fordham University, 1971.

Svensson, Frances Elizabeth. "The Concept of Change: Alternative Perspectives." Unpublished Ph.D. dissertation, University of Washington, 1970.